Business
Letters for All

Bertha J. Naterop

Erich Weis

Eva Haberfellner

OXFORD UNIVERSITY PRESS

Oxford University Press, Walton Street, Oxford OX2 6DP

OXFORD NEW YORK TORONTO
PETALING JAYA SINGAPORE HONG KONG TOKYO
DELHI BOMBAY CALCUTTA MADRAS KARACHI
NAIROBI DAR ES SALAAM CAPE TOWN
MELBOURNE AUCKLAND

and associated companies in
BERLIN IBADAN

© *Oxford University Press 1977*
Seventeenth impression 1990

Oxford, Oxford English and the Oxford English logo are
trade marks of Oxford University Press

Adapted from *Business Letters for All* ISBN 3 12 524250 9 by
Bertha J. Naterop and *Business Vocabulary for All* ISBN 3 12 524290 8
by Erich Weis and Eva Haberfellner. © Ernst Klett, Stuttgart, 1975.
Illustrations by Dennis Mallet from Hill and Mallet
Cartoons for Students of English © Oxford University Press 1972.

ISBN 0 19 580232 2

Printed in Hong Kong

Introduction

Business Letters for All is intended for students of commerce, for all those people working in business, and for those in other walks of life too. It is clear that an executive, a department manager, a salesman, a secretary or a specialist in business and technology has to write English letters, but also many people will want to buy something abroad, accept an invitation, or congratulate a friend in English. This book offers readers model letters and phrases on typical business matters, as well as on those semi-social occasions that create goodwill in international contacts. The letters cover a wide range of international business communication on both sides of the Atlantic and of the Pacific.

The main text is divided into four sections:

I. The Form of a Letter. This section deals with the formal presentation of both business and personal letters, and gives examples of British and American layouts. Examples are also given of the various acceptable ways of writing the date and the inside address, and of beginning and ending a letter. Finally, rules and hints are given on the best way of addressing an envelope.

II. Letters on Business Situations. These are model letters ranging from inquiries, quotations, sales letters, counter proposals, orders, letters giving advice of dispatch or acknowledging payment, to complaints. Several examples are included in each of these sub-sections.

III. Letters on Social Situations. These include correspondence regarding appointments and travel arrangements, invitations, thanks for hospitality, job applications, and goodwill letters.

IV. Telegrams, Telex Messages. Here, the language of the telegram and telex is dealt with. The 'do's' and 'dont's' in formulation, as well as a list of the most common abbreviations, are included.

Questions on the Letter are to be found after most of the model letters. These are intended to test the learner's understanding of the contents, and to focus his attention on the key points. Each sub-section ends with a list of model English phrases, opposite which there is space for notes, your own additions, etc.

After the main text there are some exercises on practical letter writing. Model answers are given in a key at the very end of the book.

Finally there is a lengthy business vocabulary, of some 2000 headwords enlarged with typical practical examples, expressions and compound words. It covers the following areas:

—organization of business trips
—reception of foreign business clients
—discussions of common, business, economic and technical problems
—visits to fairs, exhibitions and conferences
—dealing with every kind of business correspondence
—telephoning, telegraphing, listening to the radio
—reading of economic articles in newspapers and magazines.

The reference vocabulary is based on a careful analysis of economic and business materials such as advertisements, publicity and information material, newspaper and magazine articles, business letters. Taken into consideration equally are American and British English.

Contents

1. The Form of a Letter

a) The form of a business letter

1

RELIANCE HOLDINGS FINANCE GROUP
88 Martins Lane   London EC2V 6BH
Telephone 01-588 3782

2

Your ref: LE/N
Our ref: HCD/RP

3

14th November 19___

4

Messrs Watson & Bruce
Hardware Dealers
14 Castle Road
Edinburgh

5

Attention: Mr. P. James

6

Dear Sirs,

7

Up-to-date list of addresses

8

Thank you for your letter of 11th November, asking for an up-to-date list of addresses of our branches.

We have pleasure in enclosing this brochure, showing the location of all our branches and agencies at home and abroad.

9

Yours faithfully,

S.S. Carson

10

S.S. Carson
Group Organization
RELIANCE HOLDINGS

11

Enc.

1	**Printed letter head**	Includes name, address, telephone number of the sender, and may contain a description of the business, trade-mark, telegraphic address, telex, etc.
2	**Reference**	Initials, number or both. Addressee's reference, where known, is typed first.
3	**Date**	Abbreviations may be used for Jan. Feb. Aug. Sept. Oct. Nov. Dec. but do not write the month in figures. No mention of town.
4	**Inside address**	See page 6 and 7 for examples.
5	**Attention line**	May also be omitted.
6	**Salutation**	Starts with a capital letter and is usually followed by a comma (see also page 8).
7	**Subject line**	May also be omitted.
8	**Body of letter**	First paragraph starts with a capital letter.
9	**Complimentary Close**	Starts with capital letter, and is usually followed by a comma (see also page 8).
10	**Signature**	Followed by writer's position or status in company.
11	**Enclosure**	(if any)

---

1. Layout: British Style

b) The form of a personal letter

The writer's address does not usually include the name, which is shown by the signature.

The inside address (which may be omitted) disturbs the personal tone of the letter less when it is written in the bottom left-hand corner.

---

49 Northwick Avenue
Kenton, Middlesex
14th February, 19___

Dear Josef,

I was so sorry to have missed you when you came to London last week. I heard from my sister that you had called, but as I had joined Frank on a business trip to Amsterdam, we were out of town while you were here.

However, you will be over again in June, I hear, and we are sure to be at home then. So we look forward to seeing you next time. And don't forget—we have a spare room, and would be delighted if you made use of it.

With best wishes,

Yours sincerely,

Harry Roston

Harry Roston

Gulf Services Inc.
P.O. Box 388
Jeddah
Saudi Arabia

---

1. Layout: British Style

4

TSB TOWER
STATE
BANK

P.O. Box 2369
1314 North 38th Street
Kansas City, Kansas 66110
1-3100
January 31, 19__

Mr. George M. Cooper
2954 Wyandotte Lane
Greensleaves, Wyoming 90786

Dear Mr. Cooper:

Welcome to Tower State Bank Land!

We are pleased to learn that you have moved into the area served by Wyandotte County's newest bank. We cordially invite you to do your banking business here.

Checking and savings accounts, loans for all purposes, and complete banking services are available to you at our convenient location.

Our drive-in banking windows are open Monday through Thursday until 5:30 p.m., Friday 6:30 p.m., and Saturday from 9:30 a.m. to 12:30 p.m. Lobby hours are 9:30 a.m. to 2:00 p.m. Monday through Friday, and 3:30 p.m. to 6:30 p.m. Friday.

Plan to come in for 'eager to please' bank service.

Yours very truly,

A.J. Green

Arthur J. Green
President

AJG: bt

3. Dates and Addresses

These examples show the most widely used methods of writing dates. There is a tendency to decrease the amount of punctuation in correspondence, so that in the last few years it has become fashionable to write the date as **4 August 1976**. Also in the address, salutation and complimentary close, commas considered to be superfluous are frequently omitted.

For computer use the International Standards Organization (ISO) recommends writing the date in all-numeric form, with the year first, followed by the month and the date as 1976-08-04 or 19760804.

British style	American style
Date	
12th November, 19___ 12 November 19___ 12 Nov. 19___	November 12, 19___
Inside address (company)	
Messrs Black & Sons, 159 Knightsbridge, London SWL 87C	International Trading Company Sabas Building 507 A. Flores Street Manila Philippines
The International Trading Company 24 Churchill Avenue Maidstone, Kent ZH8 92B	The American Magazine 119 Sixth Avenue New York, NY 11011

British style	American style

Addressing an individual on company business

The Manager The Hongkong and Shanghai Banking Corporation Main Office Kuala Lumpur Malaysia	Mr. C.C. Pan Far East Jewellery Co. 68 Queen's Road East Hong Kong
Dear Sir,	Dear Sir:
Messrs Mahmoud & Son 329 Coast Road Karachi, Pakistan	The Standard Oil Company Midland Building Cleveland, Ohio 44115
For the attention of Mr. R. Singh	Attention: Mr. E.G. Glass, Jr.
Dear Sirs,	Gentlemen:

Addressing an individual on private business

T. Hardy, Esq., c/o Waltons Ltd., 230 Snow Street, Birmingham, England	Mr. C. Manzi Credito Milano Via Cavour 86 Milan Italy
Dear Tom,	Dear Mr. Manzi,
Miss Claire Waterson c/o Miller & Sons Pty. Ltd. Box 309 Sydney NSW 2000 Australia	Continental Supply Company 312 Surawongse Bangkok Thailand
	Attention: Mr. P. Wilson, Jr.
Dear Miss Waterson,	Dear Peter,

3. Dates and Addresses

4. Beginning and Ending a Letter

Every English letter needs a *salutation* (e.g. Dear Sirs) and a *complimentary close* (e.g. Yours faithfully). The only exceptions are the occasional sales letters written in 'advertising style', which may begin

'Are you sure you remembered to turn the cooker off . . .?'

a) Salutation

	British	American
Formal or Routine	Dear Sir, Dear Sirs, Dear Madam, Mesdames,	Dear Sir: Gentlemen: Dear Mr. Brown: Dear Miss Smith: Dear Mrs. Brown:
Informal	Dear Mr. Brown, Dear Miss Smith,	Dear Mr. Brown: Dear Miss Roberts:
Personal	Dear Mr. Brown, My dear Brown, Dear Jim,	Dear Mr. Brown, My dear Mr. Brown, Dear George,

b) Complimentary Close

	British	American
Formal or Routine	Yours faithfully,	Very truly yours, Sincerely yours, Yours very truly,
Informal	Yours sincerely, Yours truly,	Sincerely yours, Cordially yours,
Personal	Yours sincerely, Sincerely, With best wishes, Yours,	Sincerely yours, With kind regards, With best regards, Sincerely, Yours,

Here are a few simple rules about the best way of addressing an envelope:

1. Use separate lines for the name or company, post box or house name, number and street, town and county or city and state, postcode.

2. The number precedes the street name. Words like Street, Square, Avenue are written separately, each word starting with a capital letter.

3. Commas may be placed at the end of each line (closed punctuation), or only between city and state or county (open punctuation). Use the same form as in the letter.

4. The British *postcode* is written below the address. The American *zip code* is on the same line as city and state.

5. The postcode should always be the *last item* of information in the address, and in block capitals.

6. Whenever possible place the postcode on a *line by itself* at the end of the address.

7. When an address formerly included Postal District letters and/or numbers, these will usually be incorporated in the postcode.

8. *Do not use full stops* or any other punctuation marks between or at the end of the characters of the postcode.

9. Always leave a *clear space*, at least equivalent to one character, between the two halves of the postcode.

10. *Never underline* the postcode.

11. *Never join the characters* of a postcode in any way.

12. No writing should appear below the postcode. It is better to show return addresses on the back of an envelope rather than in the bottom corners of the front. 'For the attention of . . .' and similar messages should be shown above the address, not below it.

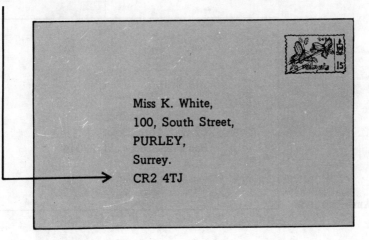

Miss K. White,
100, South Street,
PURLEY,
Surrey.
CR2 4TJ

If you use private reference numbers on letters for your own purposes, they too should be placed immediately above the address, or be kept to the upper left-hand side of the address panel.

13. Postal indications are:

Air Mail (or AIRMAIL)	Private	Sample
Express	Confidential	Fragile—with care
Urgent	To be called for	Printed matter
Registered	Please forward	

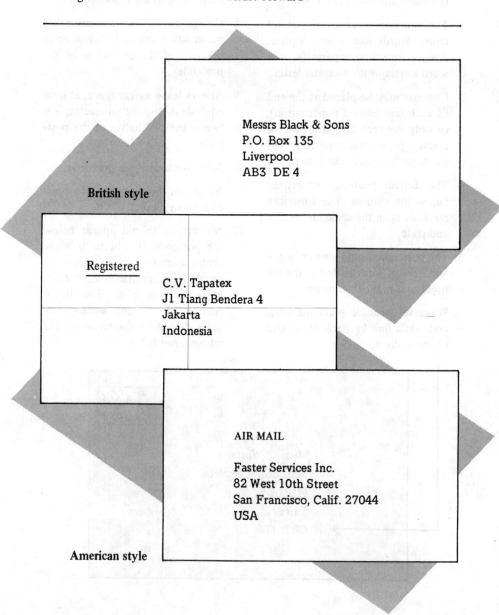

Messrs Black & Sons
P.O. Box 135
Liverpool
AB3 DE 4

British style

Registered

C.V. Tapatex
J1 Tiang Bendera 4
Jakarta
Indonesia

AIR MAIL

Faster Services Inc.
82 West 10th Street
San Francisco, Calif. 27044
USA

American style

5. Addressing an Envelope

2. Letters on Business Situations

1. Inquiries

An *inquiry* (also spelt enquiry) is sent when a businessman wants some information, especially about

- the supply of goods
- leaflets or catalogues
- quotation or prices
- samples
- terms and discounts
- availability of goods
- delivery times and deadlines
- method of transport
- insurance.

He will save unnecessary correspondence by giving full details that are relevant.

If a prospective customer approaches suppliers for the first time, it is useful to tell them something about his own business, the kind of goods he needs and for what purpose they are required. In the case of customers of long standing or repeat orders, the inquiry may be very simple. Often a phone call or a postcard will do.

'I'm sorry, sir, but Mr. Clark's very busy.'

a) Import inquiry

A Chicago businessman writes to an English manufacturer.

 MATTHEWS & WILSON
Ladies' Clothing
421 Michigan Avenue
Chicago, Ill. 60602

Messrs Grant & Clarkson
148 Mortimer Street
London W1C 37D
England

October 21, 19___

Gentlemen:

We saw your women's dresses and suits at the London Fashion Show held in New York on October 17. The lines you showed for teenagers, the 'Swinger' dresses and trouser suits, would be most suitable for our market.

Would you kindly send us your quotation for spring and summer clothing that you could supply to us by the end of January next. We would require 2,000 dresses and suits in each of the sizes 10–14, and 500 in sizes 8 and 16. Please quote c.i.f. Chicago prices. Payment is normally made by letter of credit.

Thank you for an early reply.

Very truly yours,

P. Wilson.

P. Wilson, Jr.
Buyer

Questions on the Letter

1. What do Messrs Matthews & Wilson deal in?
2. How did they hear of Messrs Grant & Clarkson?
3. Why are they interested in the 'Swinger' models?
4. What do Matthews & Wilson want a quotation for?

---

1. Inquiries

b) Domestic inquiry

A building contractor writes to a manufacturer of bathroom showers.

BUNBURY ESTATE BUILDERS
17 Fen Road
London
EC3 5AP

Central Installations
Glasgow

21st November, 19___

Dear Sirs,

With regard to your advertisement in the 'Builders' Journal' of 3rd November, we would ask you to let us have a quotation for the new bathroom showers which are described.

As building contractors we erect about a hundred houses and two or three blocks of flats a year. If your equipment is of good quality, and we receive a favourable offer, we may be able to place large orders with you.

We look forward to hearing from you soon.

Yours faithfully,

P.R. Morgan

P.R. Morgan

Questions on the Letter

1. How did Bunbury Estate Builders hear of the Central Installations Company?
2. What do they want a quotation for?
3. On what conditions will they place orders?

1. Inquiries

c) Export inquiry

An export agent writes to a manufacturer.

WD

Worldwide Dealers Ltd.

Connaught Centre
Hong Kong

The Victoria Cycle Works
P.O. Box 9271
Melbourne   June 14, 19—

Dear Sirs,

Our business agents in India have asked us for quotations for 10,000
bicycles, to be exported to Sri Lanka, India, Pakistan and Nepal.

Please let us know what quantities you are able to deliver at regular
intervals, quoting your best terms f.o.b. Brisbane. We shall handle export formalities, but would ask you to calculate container transport to
Brisbane for onward shipment.

Yours faithfully,

P. King

P. King
Asst. Export Manager

Questions on the Letter

1. Why do the Worldwide Dealers approach the Victoria Cycle Works?
2. What do they ask for apart from prices?
3. How should the bicycles be transported?

---

d) Personal inquiry

A housewife writes to the owner of a hardware store.

13 Garston Road
Bournemouth, Hants.
2nd April, 19__

Mr. S. Hampshire
Hampshire's Hardware Store
312 High Street
Bournemouth, Hants.

Dear Mr. Hampshire,

When I was in your shop this morning I looked in vain for a STIRTIP electric mixer, similar to the one I bought from you two years ago. I am so delighted with my own mixer that I would have liked to buy another one for my niece who is getting married soon. However, your assistant told me that you do not stock this make any more.

Would you please inquire if the STIRTIP mixer is still obtainable from the manufacturers. I should be obliged to you for your assistance in this matter.

Yours sincerely,

H. Marks

(Mrs.) H. Marks

Questions on the Letter

1. Why is Mrs. Marks writing to Mr. Hampshire?
2. What was Mrs. Marks told by Mr. Hampshire's assistant?
3. Who may be able to supply the mixer?

---

1. Inquiries

Phrases

Inquiries

We are retailers/importers/wholesalers in the
... trade, and would like to get in touch
with suppliers/manufacturers of ....

We have heard of your products.

Please send us prices and samples of ....

Would you please let us have a firm offer
for .../ your current catalogue showing ....

We read your advertisement.

We require ... for immediate delivery
and are interested in buying
and would like to have further details
and would like to introduce these goods

Would you kindly quote your best prices
and terms of payment for ....

What qualities are you able to supply from
stock?

We are in the market for ....

We are interested in importing ....

If your prices are competitive/If the quality
of the goods comes up to our expectations/If
the samples meet with our customers' approval we can probably let you have regular
orders.

There is a promising market here for good quality office machines, and we may be able to place large orders with you.

We look forward to receiving your quotation/prices/reply by return/as soon as possible.

Thank you in advance for any information you can give us.

An early answer would be appreciated.

We normally effect payment by letter of credit.

Payment will be made by cheque/bank transfer.

Please send us a pro-forma invoice for customs purposes.

1. Inquiries

The *quotation* in reply to an inquiry may be a simple one, containing simply the prices and other information asked for. The sales-conscious businessman, however, will take the opportunity to stimulate his correspondent's interest in his goods or services by including a sales message and the assurance that the customer will receive personal attention.

Offers are also sent without a preceding inquiry when a supplier wants to draw the attention of customers and new customers to a special product or range of goods. A *firm offer* is subject to certain conditions, a deadline for the receipt of orders, or a special price for certain quantities.

a) Export quotation: firm offer (Reply to 1a)

 GRANT & CLARKSON
148 Mortimer Street
London W1C 37D

Messrs Matthews & Wilson
421 Michigan Avenue
Chicago, Ill. 60602

Attention: Mr. P. Wilson, Jr.   30th October, 19__

Dear Sirs,

We are pleased to make you an offer regarding our 'Swinger' dresses and trouser suits in the sizes you require. Nearly all the models you saw at our fashion show are obtainable, except trouser suits in pink, of which the smaller sizes have been sold out. This line is being manufactured continuously, but will only be available again in February, so could be delivered to you in March.

All other models can be supplied by the middle of January 19__, subject to our receiving your firm order by 15th November. Our c.i.f. prices are understood to be for sea/land transport to Chicago. If you would prefer the goods to be sent by air freight, this will be charged extra at cost.

Trouser suits sizes 8–16 in white, yellow, red,
       turquoise, navy blue, black
       Sizes 12–14 also in pink   per 100 $2,650.00

Swinger dresses sizes 8—16
        in white, yellow, red, turquoise,
        black   per 100 $1,845.00

Prices: valid until 31st December, 19___
Delivery: c.i.f. Chicago
Transport: sea freight
Payment: by irrevocable letter of credit,
           or cheque with order.

You will be receiving cuttings of our materials and a colour chart. These
were airmailed to you this morning.

We hope you agree that our prices are very competitive for these good
quality clothes, and look forward to receiving your initial order.

Yours faithfully,

F.T. Burke

GRANT & CLARKSON
F.T. Burke
Export Department

Questions on the Letter

1. Which model is not obtainable at the moment?
2. When could the other models be supplied? Subject to what condition?
3. What items have already been dispatched to Matthews & Wilson? How
   and when were these sent?

'I said read it back to me, not backwards!'

---

2. Quotations, Offers

b) Enclosing quotation

Central Installations Glasgow CIG

Bunbury Estate Builders
17 Fen Road
London
EC3 5AP   24th November, 19___

Dear Sirs,

In reply to your letter of 21st November, we have pleasure in enclosing a detailed quotation for bathroom showers. Besides those advertised in the 'Builders' Journal', our illustrated catalogue also enclosed shows various types of bathroom fittings and the sizes available. Most types can be supplied from stock. 4–6 weeks should be allowed for delivery of those marked with an asterisk.

Building contractors all over Britain have found our equipment easy to install and attractive in appearance. Naturally all parts are replaceable, and our quotation includes prices of spare parts. We can allow a 2% discount on all orders of £600 in value and over, orders exceeding £2,000 are subject to 3% discount.

Any orders you place with us will be processed promptly.

Yours faithfully,

S. Stuart

S. Stuart
Sales Manager

Central Installations Glasgow

C I G

Bunbury Estate Builders
17 Fen Road
London
EC3 5AP

24th November, 19___

QUOTATION

Bathroom shower, Type G 17, length 2 ft. 6 in.	£1.20
Bathroom shower, Type G 17, length 3 ft.	£1.40
Bathroom shower, Type G 17, length 4 ft.	£1.60

Bathroom shower, Type A 42,	length 2 ft. 6 in.	£2.00
including wall bracket	length 3 ft.	£2.35
	length 4 ft.	£2.70

Parts:	Hose with protective		
	steel spiral	per foot	£0.30
	tap and shower connecting		
	rings		£0.50 each
	shower spray, type G		£0.85 each
	shower spray, type A		£1.10 each
	wall bracket, type A		£0.60 each

All prices: c.i.f. UK railway station
Terms of payment   30 days net

S. Stuart
S. Stuart
Sales Manager

Questions on the Letter

1. What is enclosed with the letter, apart from a quotation for bathroom showers?
2. Certain fittings cannot be supplied from stock. How are these indicated? How much time should be allowed for their delivery?
3. Why is the equipment made by Central Installations popular with building contractors?
4. What discount rates are quoted?
5. What makes shower A 42 more expensive?
6. Explain the terms of payment.

---

2. Quotations, Offers

21

c) Quoting terms for hotel accommodation

ATLANTIC HOTEL
10 Gresham St.
London W1

Mr. B. Yasni
Jl Kebun Karet 54
Jakarta
Indonesia

11th May, 19___

Dear Mr. Yasni,

Thank you for your letter of 1st May asking for hotel accommodation in May or June. We were pleased to hear that you wish to stay at the Altantic Hotel again during your forthcoming visit to London. Our terms are as follows:

	Bed and breakfast	Room and full board
Up to two nights		
per person, single room	£5.00	£7.50
2 persons, double room	£8.00	£12.00
Three nights or more		
per person, single room	£4.50	£7.00
2 persons, double room	£7.50	£11.50

Accommodation is still available for June, but we are almost booked up for May. We have several double rooms free from 23rd May onwards, and three single rooms for the week 26th May—3rd June. Would you therefore let us know your wishes as soon as possible, so that we can reserve the room(s) you need.

We look forward to the pleasure of seeing you here again soon.

Yours sincerely,
Reception Desk

Questions on the Letter

1. What indicates that Mr. Yasni has stayed at the Atlantic Hotel before?
2. Compare the terms quoted for up to two nights with those for three nights or more. What do you notice about the cost of the midday and evening meals?
3. What accommodation is still available in May and June?

2. Quotations, Offers

Phrases

Quotations and Offers

Thank you for your inquiry about your interest in . . . .

We are pleased to submit our lowest prices/to enclose our latest price list/for the goods you inquired about.

We can make you a firm offer for . . . .

This offer is firm subject to acceptance by . . . .

Kindly remember: this offer expires on September 30th.

Subject to prior sale.

Prices subject to change without notice.

The goods you inquired about are sold out, but we can offer you a substitute.

Please let us have your order as soon as possible, since supplies are limited.

While stocks last.

We look forward to receiving a trial order from you.

Discounts

For a quantity of 60 or more, we can allow you a special discount of 20% on the prices quoted.

The quantity discounts vary according to the size of the order.

Your initial order is subject to a special discount of 2%.

---

2. Quotations, Offers

We can grant you 3% discount on orders exceeding £100 in value/on repeat orders.

We have quoted special prices, and therefore the offer is not subject to the usual discounts.

Terms of Payment

cash in advance

cash with order (c.w.o.)

cash on delivery (c.o.d.)

Payment quarterly/monthly/at sight.

Our usual terms are cash against documents (c.a.d.)/pro-forma invoice.

We can allow you three months' credit for future orders.

As our prices are so favourable, our terms of payment are 30 days net.

Delivery

c.i.f./CIF (cost, insurance, freight)

c. & f./CF (cost and freight)

f.o.b./FOB (free on board)

f.a.s./FAS (free alongside ship)

f.o.r./FOR (free on rail)

franco domicile, free (buyer's address)

ex works/ex factory

These prices are ex warehouse.

Freight and insurance to be paid by buyer/by you.

Delivery can be made from stock/ is not included in the price.

Delivery will be made within two months of receipt of your order.

Offering Hotel Accommodation

We shall be able to accommodate all the members of your group in single or double rooms.

The rooms at the back of the hotel are very quiet.

There is an extra charge of £2 for private bathroom.

Please let us know your expected date of arrival and the duration of your stay.

We shall reserve accommodation for you accordingly.

'We do not have toothbrushes with motor-oil, sir.
Perhaps it would be better if you ordered your lunch
in English . . .'

2. Quotations, Offers

Direct advertising, in the form of letters to a selected group of readers, is an effective way to promote sales. Such *sales letters* should appeal to the potential customer. They should:

— arouse the reader's attention
— create desire to make use of your offer
— convince him that these products or services are the best ones for him
— activate him to place an order.

Almost any communication can be used as a sales letter. *Announcements* to customers and others *or important changes* can be used to make your company, your products or services better known to the public, and to attract buyers.

a) Sales letter introducing product to a new market

FARMERS FRUIT PRODUCTS
Taunton, Somerset
England

November 19___

Dear Sirs,

In the field of fruit preserves, English jams and marmalades have been regarded as the best for a century and a half. Competition has not affected their quality or attraction. Their reputation is spread by everyone who tastes them: they are recommended by word of mouth to relatives, friends and many prospective customers.

English fruit farmers supply FARMERS with the best quality produce from their orchards and gardens. Fresh citrus fruits are imported from Spain and Israel all the year round. Careful selection and preserving ensure the quality of the well-known FARMERS jams and marmalades that are supplied to stores all over the world in 1 lb jars or 2 lb tins.

Please refer to the enclosed price-list, and let us know your requirements on the form attached. You may be able to profit from special terms on your initial order. Delivery can be made shortly after we receive your order. FARMERS look forward to hearing from you soon.

Yours faithfully,

FARMERS FRUIT PRODUCTS

Enc. Price-list
      Provisional order form

Questions on the Letter

1. How long have English preserves enjoyed a widespread reputation?
2. How is their reputation spread?
3. Where does the fruit for FARMERS products come from?

b) Sales letter announcing company merger, offering a larger range of products and price reductions

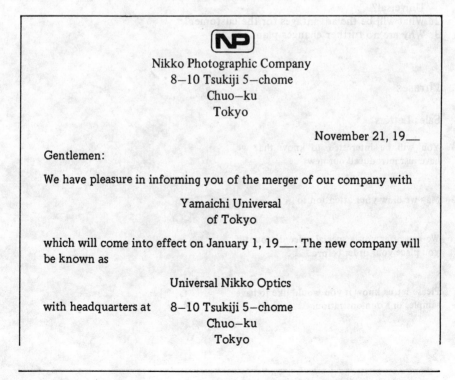

NP

Nikko Photographic Company
8—10 Tsukiji 5—chome
Chuo—ku
Tokyo

November 21, 19__

Gentlemen:

We have pleasure in informing you of the merger of our company with

Yamaichi Universal
of Tokyo

which will come into effect on January 1, 19__. The new company will be known as

Universal Nikko Optics

with headquarters at   8—10 Tsukiji 5—chome
                          Chuo—ku
                          Tokyo

3. Sales Letters, Changes in Business

Yamaichi Universal established in 1884, are well known as manufacturers of first-class optical equipment and instruments. The lenses
used in our cameras for more than sixty years have been bought from
this firm, and we look forward to closer co-operation and rationalization
of production.

As a result of this merger we are able to offer you a larger range of
cameras, projectors and optical equipment. Reduced costs in manufacture and distribution can be passed on to our customers in the form
of price reductions.

No further changes will be made. We look forward to maintaining the
personal relationship and continuing the prompt service that our customers appreciate. Please give us an opportunity of supplying you with
our extended range of goods. Our catalogue is enclosed: the choice is
yours.

                                                    Very truly yours,

Enclosure

Questions on the Letter

1. Why has the Nikko Photographic Company decided to merge with Yamaichi
   Universal?
2. What will be the advantages for the customer?
3. Why are no further changes planned?

Phrases

Sales Letters

You will be interested to know that we
have just introduced our new . . . .

May we draw your attention to . . . .

We can offer you a special price/discount if
you place your order before . . . .

Please let us know if you would like to have
samples or a demonstration.

The reputation of our products has been spread by all who know them.

We are sending you our catalogue/samples under separate cover.

Changes in business

We have pleasure in notifying you/announcing that our business has been amalgamated with . . . .

Last week we opened our new branch/factory at . . . .

To mark the occasion we are making a special offer of . . . .

We are writing to inform you that Mr. F.J. Welsh and Mr. C. Hanson have been appointed as Directors in succession to Sir Eric Seymour and Mr. J.T. Lampton.

3. Sales Letters, Changes in Business

A buyer need not accept the prices and terms offered by the seller uncondi-tionally. There will often be good reason to make a *counter-proposal* with the object of obtaining better prices or terms, or a shorter time of delivery. As a result of these negotiations the supplier could make a *concession*, particularly for an introductory sale, or if the customer places a large order.

a) Counter-proposal

Roberts Import Company

Av. Rio Branco 278
Grupo 506
Rio de Janeiro

Farmers Fruit Products
Taunton, Somerset
England   16th November, 19___

Dear Sirs,

Thank you for your letter of 10th November, enclosing your price-list.
The 2 lb tins of marmalade would not be suitable for our customers,
but we should like to buy 15,000 1 lb jars. However, there is one dis-advantage when compared with local produce. Housewives here are
used to a jar containing 500 grammes; the English pound is only 454
grammes. Therefore would ask you to reduce the prices quoted for
quality A2 by ten per cent.

As far as settlement is concerned, we would suggest paying half the
amount against your invoice on receipt of the goods, and the second
half within 30 days, deducting two per cent discount.

The samples arrived yesterday, and we must admit that your marma-lade is delicious. Would you kindly let us know as soon as possible if
you can supply us on the terms mentioned.

Yours faithfully,

1. Why does English marmalade seem expensive to Brazilian buyers?
2. What price reduction do they ask for?
3. What terms of payment do they suggest?

b) Reply to counter-proposal

FARMERS FRUIT PRODUCTS
Taunton, Somerset
England

Roberts Import Company
Av. Rio Branco 278
Grupo 506
Rio de Janeiro   22nd November, 19——

Dear Sirs,

   We have carefully considered the proposals you made in your letter
of 16th November.

   It would give us great pleasure to supply you with the marmalade
you wish to order. You have noticed that its quality is probably better
than that of the marmalade usually sold in your country. You will soon
see that your customers notice the difference too, and will want to
place repeat orders.

   We should like to prove this to you, and are therefore prepared to
grant you a special discount of 5% for the quantity of 15,000 jars of
A2 orange marmalade. This, with the 2% cash discount which we would
allow, should enable you to offer the goods for sale at competitive
prices.

   May we look forward to receiving your order? We assure you of our
best attention.

                                      Yours faithfully,

                                      Robert R. Wilson.

                                      Robert R. Wilson

4. Counter-proposals, Concessions

Questions on the Letter

1. Why do FARMERS think that customers in Brazil are likely to place repeat orders?
2. What discounts are they willing to allow?

Phrases

Counter-proposals

Your offer was disappointing; we had expected better terms.

The products you sell are not suitable for our market unless . . . .

We can only consider placing an order if you can give us a price reduction of 10%.

As far as payment is concerned, we usually do business on a 3 months' credit basis.

We trust you can see your way clear to making us a price concession.

Concessions

We agree to making a reduction in price if this will help you to develop your market for our products.

In reply to your request, we are willing to allow you an extra discount of 20% on this order/ a longer credit period.

Since we should like to enter the market in your country, we have cut our margin of profit to give you the benefit of a 4% reduction.

In comparison to the correspondence so far, *placing an order* is simple from the point of view of letter-writing. Very often the purchasing department or the buyer fills in an order form, although he may prefer to write a letter to make certain points quite clear. There could be special import regulations which make it necessary to complete formalities, or he may want to stress delivery instructions or other matters.

The supplier sends an *order acknowledgement* promptly, to thank his customer for the order. If prices or delivery times have changed, the customer must be notified. If the goods ordered are no longer available, a substitute may be offered.

The Economist

The international briefing for responsible people

Brief yourself on the central issues in business and politics with THE ECONOMIST. It is hard to read up a country or an unfamiliar field at the last minute. This is where regular reading of THE ECONOMIST pays off.

Subscription order form

Please enter a subscription for one year

UK	£20.00
Europe *airspeeded*	US $50.00
USA & Canada *airspeeded*	US $50.00
Rest of world airspeeded	US $59.00
Rest of world surface mail	US $42.00
(Copies take between 3–8 weeks)	
Quarterly Index extra	US $ 9.00

☐ I enclose my cheque for

(£ Sterling, Canadian $ and Eurocheques can be accepted at the current exchange rates).

My name
BLOCK LETTERS PLEASE

My address

9 W V U T S R Q P N

Please send this entire order form, together with your remittance, to: The Economist Newspaper Limited, Subscription Department, PO Box 190 23A St. James's Street, London SW1A 1HF, England

Bank transfer form

(For some countries the bank transfer service may be a more convenient method of payment).

Please enter the name and address of your bank and send this complete order form to The Economist. We will enter your subscription and then arrange for your bank to transfer payment from your account. Please do not send direct to your bank.

Name of your bank

Address

Please transfer to The Economist Newspaper Limited A/C No. 30341584 Barclays Bank Limited 23 St. James's Street London SW1A 1HE, England	The £ sterling equivalent of US $	and debit the following account
	Name	
	Account no	Signature
	Date	

Bank only: Important – please quote this reference when crediting The Economist account   Ref:

Registered Office 25 St. James's Street, London SW1A 1HG Registered in London Number 236383

---

a) Enclosing printed order form

Roberts Import Company

Av. Rio Branco 278
Grupo 506
Rio de Janeiro

ric

Farmers Fruit Products
Taunton, Somerset
England

30th November, 19___

Dear Sirs,

Our Order for Marmalade

In reply to your letter of 22nd November, we thank you for allowing
us a special discount. This makes it possible for us to place an order
and to expect quite good sales.

We have pleasure in enclosing our Order No. 732/AS, and would ask
you to return the duplicate to us, duly signed, as an acknowledgement.

Yours faithfully,

Carlos Santos

Enc. Order No. 732/AS

Roberts Import Company

**Av. Rio Branco 278
Grupo 506
Rio de Janeiro**

ORDER

No. 732/AS
(Please quote this
number on all
correspondence)

Farmers Fruit Products
Taunton, Somerset
England

30th November, 19___

Please supply

Quantity	Unit	Description	Currency and price
15,000	1 lb jars	Orange marmalade quality A2	Cruzerios 3.5 each

Delivery:	by 10th December, 19___
Method of transport:	Shipment
Marks:	RIC
	SP
Payment:	Half the amount on receipt of consignment, remainder within 30 days
Discount:	5% special discount
	2% cash discount

p.p. Chief Buyer

Roberts Import Company

Please sign the duplicate of this order and return it to us as an acknowledgement.

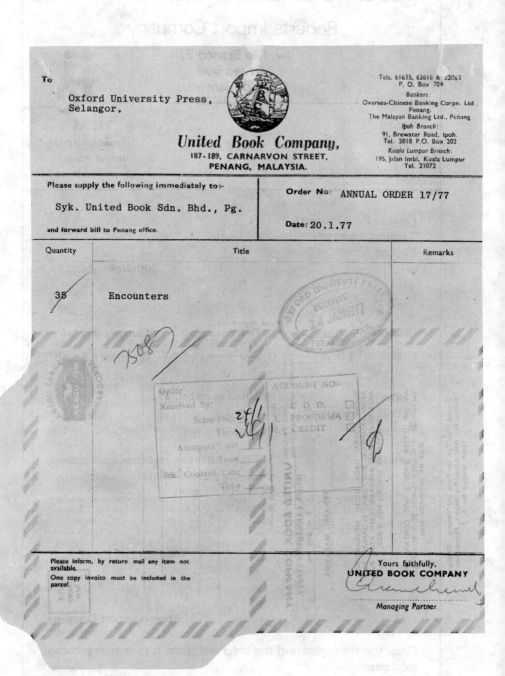

To

Oxford University Press,
Selangor.

Tels. 61635, 63616 & 22063
P. O. Box 704

Bankers:
Oversea-Chinese Banking Corpn. Ltd.,
Penang.
The Malayan Banking Ltd., Penang

Ipoh Branch:
91, Brewster Road, Ipoh.
Tel. 2818 P.O. Box 202

Kuala Lumpur Branch:
195, Jalan Imbi, Kuala Lumpur
Tel. 23072

United Book Company,
187-189, CARNARVON STREET,
PENANG, MALAYSIA.

Please supply the following immediately to:-

Syk. United Book Sdn. Bhd., Pg.

and forward bill to Penang office.

Order No: ANNUAL ORDER 17/77

Date: 20.1.77

Quantity	Title	Remarks
35	Encounters	

Order
Received By:
Sales Date
Time
Accounts Date
Time
Stk. Control Date
Time

ACCOUNT NO:-
C.O.D. ☐
PROFORMA ☐
CREDIT

Please inform, by return mail any item not available.

One copy invoice must be included in the parcel.

Yours faithfully,
UNITED BOOK COMPANY

....
Managing Partner.

b) Enclosing an acknowledgement

 FARMERS FRUIT PRODUCTS
Taunton, Somerset
England

Roberts Import Company
Av. Rio Branco 278
Grupo 506
Rio de Janeiro   8th December, 19___

Dear Sirs,

Thank you very much for your Order No. 732/AS dated 30th November, 19___. As requested we enclose the copy, duly signed, as order acknowledgement.

Our dispatch department is processing your order today, and will let you know when the consignment will reach you.

We confidently hope that you will have a good turnover, and that you will be able to place repeat orders with us in the near future.

                                                        Yours faithfully,

Enc.

Questions on the Letter

1. What are FARMERS sending as an acknowledgement of the order?
2. How will Roberts Import Company know when the marmalade is going to arrive?
3. Why do FARMERS write a letter with the acknowledgement?

c) Making a hotel reservation

                                                   Aztec Press
                                                   Adolfo Prieto 936
                                                   Col. del Valle
                                                   Mexico 12. D.F.

The Manager
Atlantic Hotel
London W1   13 May 19___

Dear Sir,

Six members of our staff will be coming to London on business from 28th May to 1st June. Would you therefore please reserve the following accommodation for five nights:

5. Orders, Order Acknowledgements

2 single rooms
2 double rooms   for bed and breakfast.

As my wife will be joining me in London on Saturday, 2nd June, I shall need

1 double room with bed and breakfast

for this date. Please bill this accommodation to me at my private address as above.

Although the group will arrive in London by rail at 10.13 a.m., we have meetings until the late afternoon and will probably check in at about 7 p.m.

Please confirm this booking.

Yours faithfully,

Philip Cooper

Philip Cooper

d) Import order

MATTHEWS & WILSON
Ladies' Clothing
421 Michigan Avenue
Chicago, Ill. 60602

Messrs Grant & Clarkson
148 Mortimer Street
London W1C 37D
                                   November 4, 19___

Gentlemen:

Thank you for your quotation of October 30. We have pleasure in placing an order with you for

2,100 'Swinger' dresses   at Price: $38,745

in the colours and sizes specified below:

Quantity	Size	Colour
50	8, 16	White
100	10, 12, 14	White
50	8, 16	Turquoise
100	10, 12, 14	Turquoise
50	8, 16	Red
100	10, 12, 14	Red

50	16	Yellow
100	10, 12, 14	Yellow
50	16	Black
100	10, 12, 14	Black

Delivery: air freight, c.i.f. Chicago.

We shall open a letter of credit with your bank as soon as we receive your order acknowledgement. Please arrange for immediate collection and transport, since we need the dresses for Christmas.

Very truly yours,

P. Wilson.

P. Wilson, Jr.
Buyer

Questions on the Letter

1. Which are the most popular sizes?
2. How should delivery be made?
3. How will payment be made?
4. Why must the clothes be delivered immediately?

e) Exchange of cables

MATWIS CHICAGO	8 NOVEMBER

YOUR ORDER 4 NOVEMBER PLEASE CONFIRM QUANTITY 2100 SWINGER ORDERED STOP SPECIFICATION 1900 ONLY

GRANT CLARKSON LONDON

GRANT CLARKSON LONDON	9 NOVEMBER

REGRET CLERICAL ERROR OUR ORDER IS FOR 1900 SWINGER DRESSES AS SPECIFIED PRICE $35,055 PLEASE CONFIRM

MATWIS CHICAGO

Questions

1. Why do Grant & Clarkson query the quantity of dresses ordered?
2. How do you think the mistake occurred?
3. Why do both companies cable 'please confirm'?

5. Orders, Order Acknowledgements

f) Confirmation

 GRANT & CLARKSON
148 Mortimer Street
London W1C 37D

Messrs Matthews & Wilson
421 Michigan Avenue
Chicago, Ill. 60602

Attention: Mr. P. Wilson, Jr.   9th November, 19___

Dear Sirs,

Thank you for your order dated 4th November. On checking it we noticed a discrepancy between the first paragraph and the quantities you specified, and therefore cabled you yesterday as follows:

> YOUR ORDER 4 NOVEMBER PLEASE CONFIRM QUANTITY
> 2100 SWINGER ORDERED STOP SPECIFICATION 1900 ONLY

Today we received your cable in reply reading:

> REGRET CLERICAL ERROR OUR ORDER IS FOR 1900 SWINGER
> DRESSES AS SPECIFIED PRICE $35,055 PLEASE CONFIRM

We have pleasure in confirming that we have booked your order for 1900 'Swinger' dresses. Air shipment can be made as soon as we receive confirmation that a letter of credit has been opened for the amount mentioned above.

Please note that our quotation of 30th October was for sea freight c.i.f. Chicago. Naturally we can arrange for the goods to be sent as air cargo, but as this is more expensive we shall have to charge you for the extra costs. In this way, however, you will certainly receive the goods within a week, thus enabling you to distribute them in time for Christmas.

Yours faithfully,

F.T.Burke

GRANT & CLARKSON
F.T. Burke
Export Department

Questions on the Letter

1. What discrepancy does the letter refer to?
2. Why are both cables quoted in the letter?
3. When can the goods be dispatched?
4. Why will Matthews & Wilson have to pay more for freight?

---

5. Orders, Order Acknowledgements

Phrases

Placing of Orders

Please supply/send us the undermentioned goods.

With reference to your quotation, we enclose our order for immediate delivery.

We can accept your offer on these terms, and are pleased to place an order for . . . .

As the goods are urgently required, we should be grateful for delivery by . . . .

Please confirm that you can supply this quantity by the required date.

If any items are out of stock, please submit a quotation for a substitute.

Acknowledgement of Orders

We are pleased to acknowledge your order for . . . .

Your order is already being carried out/ executed/processed, and delivery will be made in accordance with your instructions.

We confirm that delivery will be made by March 15th, as requested.

Delivery will be made immediately on receipt of your cheque/remittance/letter of credit.

We trust that this initial order will lead to further dealings between our two companies.

Refusal of Orders

We regret to inform you that the goods ordered are out of stock/no longer available.

We can offer you a substitute which is the same price and of similar quality to the goods ordered.

---

5. Orders, Order Acknowledgements

6. Dispatch, Packing, Transport

a) Advice of dispatch

 FARMERS FRUIT PRODUCTS
Taunton, Somerset
England

Roberts Import Company
Av. Rio Branco 278
Grupo 506
Rio de Janeiro

Ref: Your Order No. 732/AS of 26th November

18th December, 19___

Dear Sirs,

We are pleased to advise you that the marmalade you ordered was dispatched by rail this morning. In spite of every care in packing, it sometimes happens that a few jars are broken in transit. Should there be any breakages or other cause for complaint, please do not hesitate to let us know.

The goods are being consigned via Southampton for shipment by MV Orion arriving at Sao Paulo on 22nd January. Further details, including packing and marks, are contained in our invoice No. 20015 enclosed in duplicate. We look forward to receiving your first payment by bank transfer or cheque.

We trust that our marmalade will sell well in your country.

Yours faithfully,

Dispatch Department

Enc. Invoice No. 20015

Questions on the Letter

1. How was the consignment dispatched?
2. How will it be forwarded?
3. What is its destination?
4. What details are there in an invoice? (List five items.)

b) Packing

Victoria Cycle Works

P.O. Box 9271 · Melbourne · Australia

Worldwide Dealers Ltd.
Connaught Centre
Hong Kong

Attention: Mr. P. King

1st August, 19__

Dear Sirs,

The 10,000 cycles you ordered will be ready for dispatch by 17th August next. Since you require them for onward shipment to Sri Lanka, India, Pakistan and Nepal, we are arranging for them to be packed in seaworthy containers.

Each bicycle is enclosed in a corrugated cardboard pack, and 20 are banded together and wrapped in sheet plastic. A container holds 240 cycles; the whole cargo would therefore comprise 42 containers, each weighing 8 tons. Dispatch can be made from our works by rail to be forwarded from Brisbane harbour. The freight charges from works f.o.b. Brisbane are A$60 per container, total A$2,520 for this consignment, excluding container hire, which will be charged to your account.

Please let us have your delivery instructions.

Yours faithfully,

N. Foster

Neil Foster

Questions on the Letter

1. Why must the cycles be packed in seaworthy containers for transport from Melbourne to Brisbane?
2. What are the advantages of container packing?
3. Who pays for freight?
4. Who pays for container hire?

---

6. Dispatch, Packing, Transport

c) Air shipment

 GRANT & CLARKSON
148 Mortimer Street
London W1C 37D

Messrs Matthews & Wilson
421 Michigan Avenue
Chicago, Ill. 60602

20th November, 19___

Dear Sirs,

We have pleasure in notifying you that your credit was confirmed by
our bank yesterday, 19th November. We have had the 1900 'Swinger'
dresses collected today for transport by British Airways to Chicago on
25th November.

Enclosed is our invoice for the goods in question plus the extra charges
for air freight, packing lists to facilitate customs clearance at your end,
certificate of origin, air waybill and insurance policy.

Hoping that this initial order will lead to further business, we are

Yours faithfully,

Questions on the Letter

1. Why could dispatch only be made on 20th November?
2. Why was air freight charged extra? (See also letter p. 40).
3. What documents are necessary for an air shipment?

6. Dispatch, Packing, Transport

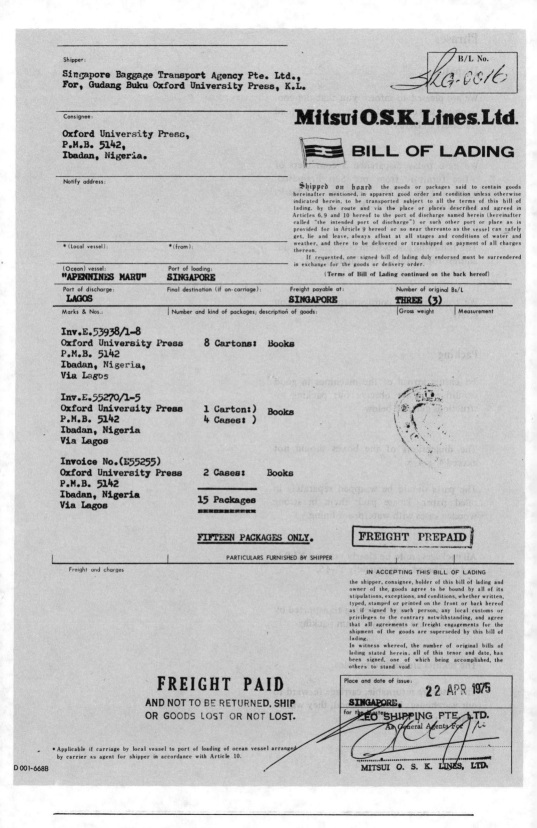

Phrases

Dispatch

We are pleased to inform you that the consignment was collected this morning for road transport to Derby.

We have today dispatched 3 containers of office furniture from our San Francisco warehouse against your order no. __. Marks and numbers UN-SW 1–3.

The following goods were consigned to your address for arrival on 3rd January next.

We trust that the consignment reaches you safely.

Packing

To ensure arrival of the machines in good condition, please observe our packing instructions detailed below.

The dimensions of the boxes should not exceed $4' \times 4' \times 2' 6''$.

The parts should be wrapped separately in oiled paper. Please pack them in strong wooden cases with waterproof lining.

All packages are to be clearly marked XLP 1, and numbered consecutively 1–15.

Since these articles are being transported by air, we will use light styrofoam packing.

The textiles are packed in bales.

The cases are returnable, carriage forward to our warehouse. If not returned, they will be charged at $3.50 each.

Shipping Documents

The shipping documents have been sent to the Mercantile Bank Inc., New York, with a sight draft for $7,000.

We enclose packing lists, bill of lading, invoice, certificate of origin and import licence.

The shipping documents will be sent to you by our forwarders.

Would you kindly pay the freight and/or warehousing charges and debit them to our account.

Non-arrival

Contrary to your Advice Note 4328 of 8th April, the consignment scheduled for arrival here on 14th May still has not reached us.

Since we received no forwarding instructions, we have had to warehouse the goods, otherwise the carriers would have returned them.

Four bags were missing from the consignment delivered to us on 14th November. Please look into this matter immediately.

'Psst! What time's the next collection?'

---

6. Dispatch, Packing, Transport

Customers usually settle their accounts by cheque when payment is due, according to the terms of payment. However, some overlook the date and have to be reminded of the amount outstanding. The first letter is written in a friendly tone, as the delay may have been due to an oversight. When *payment* has not been received in reply to this *reminder*, the creditor will write again in a firmer tone. If the debtor gives no reason for non-payment and sends no remittance, the last course is to use the services of a collection agency or to take legal action.

There may be good reasons for a customer's inability to pay. Where possible he should at least make a part payment, and agree to settle the balance of his account within a reasonable time.

a) Making payment

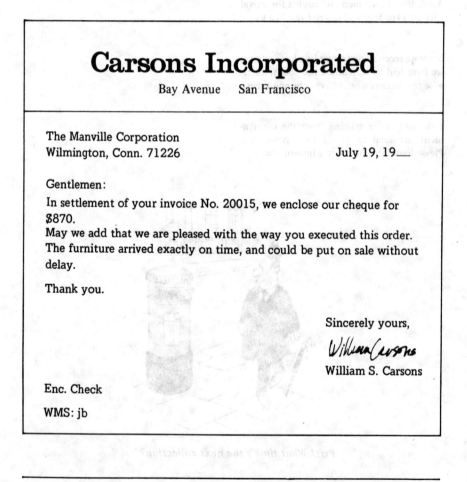

Carsons Incorporated

Bay Avenue   San Francisco

The Manville Corporation
Wilmington, Conn. 71226

July 19, 19___

Gentlemen:

In settlement of your invoice No. 20015, we enclose our cheque for $870.
May we add that we are pleased with the way you executed this order. The furniture arrived exactly on time, and could be put on sale without delay.

Thank you.

Sincerely yours,

William Carsons

William S. Carsons

Enc. Check

WMS: jb

Questions on the Letter

1. How do Carsons make their payment?
2. What is Carsons' reaction to the way the order was carried out?

b) Acknowledging payment

THE MANVILLE CORPORATION
Wilmington, Conn. 71226

Carsons Inc.
Bay Avenue
San Francisco   July 22, 19___

Dear Mr. Carsons:

We were pleased to receive your check for $870. It has been credited to your account, which is now completely clear.

Please give us the opportunity of serving you again in any way we can.

Sincerely yours,

Robert L. Thompson

Enc. Receipt

HG: et

Questions on the Letter

1. What is the state of Carsons' account after this payment?
2. What do the Manville Corporation enclose with the letter?

---

7. Payment and Reminders

c) **Reminder**

TTG Industries

550 Broad Street
Harrisburg, Pa. 17105

Mandarin Importing & Exporting Co.
No. 64 Market Street
Singapore 1.

February 6, 19___

Gentlemen:

We would like to draw your attention to the enclosed statement, which shows a balance in our favour of $3,750 as at December 31, 19___. May we remind you that our terms are 30 days net.

Kindly send us your remittance as soon as possible. Should you however have settled the account since this letter was written, please disregard our reminder.

Very truly yours,

Mary J. Adams

Credit Department

Questions on the Letter

1. How long was payment overdue when this reminder was written?
2. What should Mandarin Importing & Exporting Co. do if they have settled their account in the meantime?

---

d) Second notice

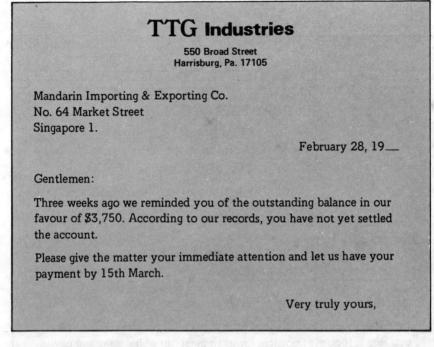

TTG Industries

**550 Broad Street
Harrisburg, Pa. 17105**

Mandarin Importing & Exporting Co.
No. 64 Market Street
Singapore 1.

February 28, 19__

Gentlemen:

Three weeks ago we reminded you of the outstanding balance in our favour of $3,750. According to our records, you have not yet settled the account.

Please give the matter your immediate attention and let us have your payment by 15th March.

Very truly yours,

Questions on the Letter

1. Why are TTG writing to Mandarin Importing & Exporting Co. again?
2. How long are TTG Industries prepared to wait?

e) Final notice

March 20, 19__

Gentlemen:

We have asked you repeatedly to settle your outstanding account for $3,750. Unfortunately we have received neither a reply from you nor your remittance.

Unless we receive your payment by March 31, 19__ we shall be compelled to place the matter in the hands of our lawyer. As such a step would damage your credit standing, we sincerely hope you will send us your check immediately.

Very truly yours,

Questions on the Letter

1. What do you notice about the tone of this final notice?
2. What should Mandarin Importing & Exporting Co. have done?
3. How could legal action damage their reputation?

7. Payment and Reminders

f) Request for extension of credit

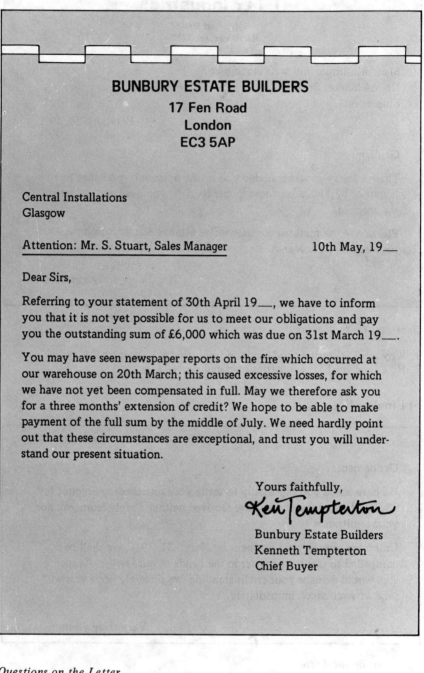

BUNBURY ESTATE BUILDERS
17 Fen Road
London
EC3 5AP

Central Installations
Glasgow

Attention: Mr. S. Stuart, Sales Manager   10th May, 19___

Dear Sirs,

Referring to your statement of 30th April 19___, we have to inform
you that it is not yet possible for us to meet our obligations and pay
you the outstanding sum of £6,000 which was due on 31st March 19___.

You may have seen newspaper reports on the fire which occurred at
our warehouse on 20th March; this caused excessive losses, for which
we have not yet been compensated in full. May we therefore ask you
for a three months' extension of credit? We hope to be able to make
payment of the full sum by the middle of July. We need hardly point
out that these circumstances are exceptional, and trust you will understand our present situation.

Yours faithfully,

Ken Tempterton

Bunbury Estate Builders
Kenneth Tempterton
Chief Buyer

Questions on the Letter

1. Why can't Bunbury Estate Builders meet their obligations?
2. How long do they think it will take them to pay off the balance?

7. Payment and Reminders

52

g) Extending credit

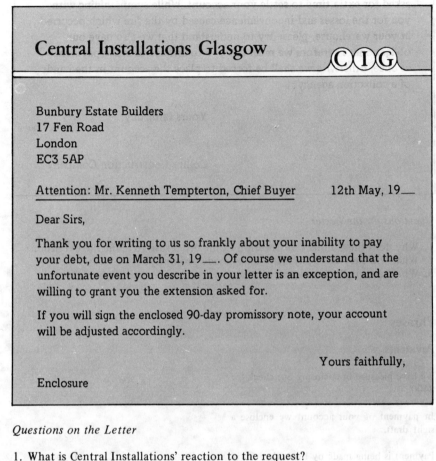

Central Installations Glasgow **CIG**

Bunbury Estate Builders
17 Fen Road
London
EC3 5AP

Attention: Mr. Kenneth Tempterton, Chief Buyer   12th May, 19__

Dear Sirs,

Thank you for writing to us so frankly about your inability to pay
your debt, due on March 31, 19__. Of course we understand that the
unfortunate event you describe in your letter is an exception, and are
willing to grant you the extension asked for.

If you will sign the enclosed 90-day promissory note, your account
will be adjusted accordingly.

                                                          Yours faithfully,

Enclosure

Questions on the Letter

1. What is Central Installations' reaction to the request?
2. How do they extend the terms of payment?

h) Refusing extension

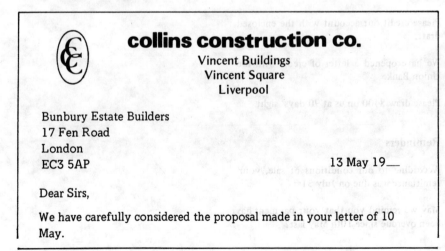

collins construction co.

Vincent Buildings
Vincent Square
Liverpool

Bunbury Estate Builders
17 Fen Road
London
EC3 5AP   13 May 19__

Dear Sirs,

We have carefully considered the proposal made in your letter of 10
May.

7. Payment and Reminders

There have, however, been several instances in the past when you have asked for extra time to settle your account. While sympathizing with you for the losses and inconvenience caused by the fire which occurred at your warehouse, please try to understand that we also have our obligations. Therefore we must ask you to arrange to make payment at once, otherwise we shall be forced to place the account in the hands of a collection agency.

Yours faithfully,

Collins Construction Company

Questions on the Letter

1. Why does the Collins Construction Company refuse to grant the extension?
2. What will they do if payment is not made promptly?
3. What can a collection agency do?

Phrases

Payments

We have pleasure in enclosing our check for $400.

In payment of your account we enclose a sight draft.

Payment is being made by banker's draft in settlement of your invoice for $400.

The Union Bank will accept your draft on our behalf.

Please credit our account with the enclosed draft.

We have opened a letter of credit with the Union Bank.

Please draw $400 on us at 90 days' sight.

Reminders

According to our conditions of sale, your remittance was due on July 31st.

May we remind you that your payment has been overdue since 10th May last?

It is no doubt through an oversight on your part that settlement is two months overdue.

We must insist on receiving payment by 31st March; failing this we shall be compelled to take legal action.

We have frequently reminded you of the outstanding amount, but have received no reply or remittance from you.

Extension of Credit

Due to poor weather conditions, business has been dull.

Sales have dropped recently, leaving us in financial difficulties.

The recent devaluation of the dollar has caused a setback in business.

Would you allow me to postpone settlement of your account?

We suggest making a part payment of $200 now, and paying the balance by September 20th.

Since you have always met your obligations in the past, we are prepared to allow you a postponement of payment.

Please send us half of the amount by return, and sign the enclosed acceptance for the remainder.

Since our profit is marginal, we cannot grant exceptions to our terms of payment.

Your failure to pay on time is in turn causing us financial embarrassment.

We trust you will settle the remainder by paying in monthly instalments.

7. Payment and Reminders

8. Complaints, Handling Complaints

Mistakes may occur in day-to-day business, and these give cause for *complaint*. There might have been a misunderstanding about the goods to be supplied; perhaps the warehouse clerk made an error in addressing the parcels; sometimes a consignment is dispatched too late or delays are caused in transit; damage may have occurred during delivery; a manufacturing defect is discovered when a machine is used. The customer is understandably annoyed, yet this is no reason to write an angry letter of complaint. He will get better results if he takes the trouble to explain his complaint clearly, and to propose ways in which matters can be put right. His company may make mistakes too: firms often have to manage with insufficiently trained personnel or to contend with a staff shortage, so mistakes and accidents happen.

It is particularly necessary to exercise tact in *handling complaints*. A disappointed customer cannot be put off with mere apologies—he is entitled to know how the mistake will be remedied: when he will receive the goods ordered; what he is to do with the wrong consignment or the damaged goods he received; when he will receive a replacement for his defective machine, or if it can be repaired quickly.

a) Complaint

From Matthews & Wilson to Grant & Clarkson

· November 22, 19___

Gentlemen:

Thank you for your delivery of 'Swinger' dresses, which we ordered on November 4. However, we wish to draw your attention to two matters.

Of the red dresses supplied, one lot of 100 (size 12) included clothes of a lighter red than the other sizes. Since we deliver a collection of various sizes to each store, it would be obvious to customers that the clothes are dissimilar. In addition, the red belt supplied does not match these dresses. We are returning two of these by separate mail, and would ask you to replace the whole lot by 100 dresses size 12 in the correct colour.

As far as your charges for air freight are concerned, we agreed to pay the extra costs which you invoiced. However, your costs for packing

---

and insurance must have been lower for air cargo, and we request you to take this fact into consideration and to make an adjustment to the invoice amount. Would you please send us a rectified invoice, reduced accordingly.

We look forward to your dealing with these questions without delay.

Very truly yours,

Questions on the Letter

1. Why are the dresses unsatisfactory?
2. Why would this be obvious to customers?
3. What do Matthews & Wilson ask Grant & Clarkson to do?
4. Why do freight charges seem too high?
5. What adjustment do Matthews & Wilson want made?

'Now we'll see whether that expensive French Course on gramophone records was worth the money or not, George!'

8. Complaints, Handling Complaints

b) Handling a complaint

From Grant & Clarkson to Matthews & Wilson

2nd December, 19___

Dear Sirs,

The colour of the dresses about which you complain is indeed lighter than it should be. Apparently this was overlooked by the controller responsible. Please accept our apologies for the oversight.

We are sending you a new lot by air this week, and would ask you to return the faulty clothes at your convenience, carriage forward. Alternatively you may keep this lot for sale as seconds at a reduced price of $1,120.

You are perfectly correct in saying that packing and insurance costs are normally less for cargo sent by air. May we remind you, however, that in this case your request to send the goods by air was made at very short notice. It was not possible for us to use the lighter air freight packing materials, as most of the dresses were ready for shipment by sea freight (please see our letter of 9th November). Furthermore, our insurance is on an open policy at a flat rate, and depends on the value of the goods, not the method of transport. For these reasons our invoice No. 14596 dated 15th November 19___ is still valid, and we look forward to receiving your remittance when due.

Yours faithfully,

Questions on the Letter

1. How do Grant & Clarkson explain the fact that the dresses are of a lighter colour?
2. How do they deal with the complaint?
3. Why don't they comply with the request to reduce the invoice amount?

---

8. Complaints, Handling Complaints

58

c) Answering a complaint about poor service

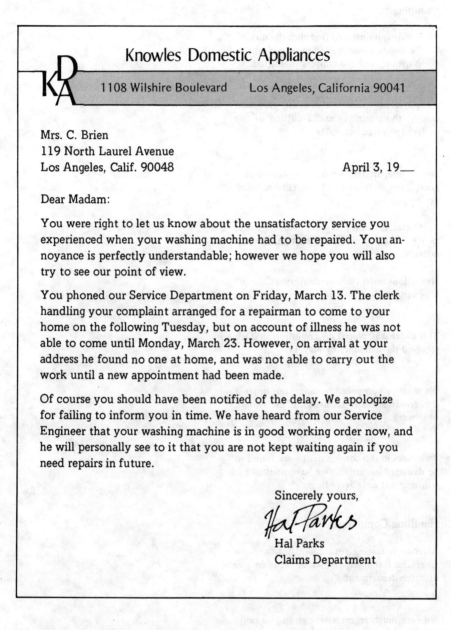

Knowles Domestic Appliances

1108 Wilshire Boulevard   Los Angeles, California 90041

Mrs. C. Brien
119 North Laurel Avenue
Los Angeles, Calif. 90048   April 3, 19___

Dear Madam:

You were right to let us know about the unsatisfactory service you experienced when your washing machine had to be repaired. Your annoyance is perfectly understandable; however we hope you will also try to see our point of view.

You phoned our Service Department on Friday, March 13. The clerk handling your complaint arranged for a repairman to come to your home on the following Tuesday, but on account of illness he was not able to come until Monday, March 23. However, on arrival at your address he found no one at home, and was not able to carry out the work until a new appointment had been made.

Of course you should have been notified of the delay. We apologize for failing to inform you in time. We have heard from our Service Engineer that your washing machine is in good working order now, and he will personally see to it that you are not kept waiting again if you need repairs in future.

Sincerely yours,

Hal Parks

Hal Parks
Claims Department

Questions on the Letter

1. What did Mrs. Brien complain about?
2. Why couldn't the repairman come on time?
3. Why wasn't there anyone at home when the repairman called?
4. What personal attention do Knowles promise Mrs. Brien?

8. Complaints, Handling Complaints

Phrases

Complaints

We are disappointed to find that the quality of the goods you supplied does not correspond with that of the samples submitted.

To prove our statement we are enclosing one of these samples and a cutting of the material received yesterday.

We are prepared to retain these unsuitable goods, but only at a substantially reduced price.

This delay is causing us great inconvenience, as we have promised our customers early delivery.

Please look into the non-delivery of the 20 typewriters which we ordered on April 19th.

This order was placed on condition that we received the machines by May 1st.

We shall be compelled to cancel our order if the goods are not received by the end of next week.

Two cases in the consignment were found to be damaged on arrival. We have marked the consignment note accordingly.

Handling Complaints

After investigating your complaint, we have ascertained that an error was made in our dispatch department.

We very much regret having given you cause for complaint.

Steps are being taken immediately to ensure that such mistakes do not occur in future.

Please accept our sincere apologies for this delay and the trouble it has caused you.

Since this delay is beyond our control, we cannot assume any liability.

Your claim has been passed on to our insurance company, who will get in touch with you soon.

We apologize for the delay and enclose our credit note/rectified invoice.

A replacement for the faulty equipment was dispatched today.

If you keep the damaged goods, we are prepared to invoice them at 50% of the list price.

'And STOP telling everybody you only cost me ten pence.'

---

8. Complaints, Handling Complaints

3. Letters on Social Situations

1. Appointments and Travel Arrangements

Leaving correspondence on the exchange of goods, services and money, let us have a look at the more personal side. In personal meetings, talks take priority over writing, yet *appointments* and *travel arrangements* often involve correspondence. Even if appointments have been made verbally it is wise to confirm them in writing, as a letter is clearer to all parties concerned than a telephone message, where it is easy to misinterpret dates and places.

Travel arrangements can, of course, be made without writing letters, However, correspondence is necessary if accommodation is to be booked abroad, or if one is to travel further from places outside one's own country.

'Er—could you please tell us the way to the nearest bus-stop?'

1. Appointments and Travel Arrangements

a) Making an appointment

International Import Corporation

44 Nasatar St.
Cairo

18 August, 19___

Dear Mr. Carter,

As mentioned in my letter of 9 August, I am planning to spend a few days in London next month, on my way to the United States. The dates are now settled: I shall arrive at Heathrow on Wednesday, 3 September (Flight BA 602 15 30) and leave on Friday night. I shall be staying at the Cumberland Hotel, Marble Arch, London W1.

On 3 September I already have some appointments, but could come to your office any time on Thursday, 4 September. Would you kindly leave a message at my hotel letting me know what time would suit you.

One of the most important matters to be discussed is the percentage of commission you could give us for distributing your SELECT copier in Egypt. As we have already indicated, 10% is unacceptable to us: we require at least 12% if we are to do a good job of selling this equipment in Egypt.

In the hope that we can come to terms, and looking forward to meeting you, I am,

Yours sincerely,

Amir Hanna

INTERNATIONAL IMPORT CORPORATION
Amir Hanna

Mr. John Carter, Export Manager
Business Machines Ltd.
39 Broad Street
London EC4

Questions on the Letter

1. When did Mr. Hanna previously notify Mr. Carter of his visit?
2. When does he suggest they meet?
3. How will the time be fixed?
4. What does Mr. Hanna want to discuss with the London firm?

---

1. Appointments and Travel Arrangements

b) Expressing regret at having missed someone

SCANDIA CORPORATION
Nyelandsvej 20   Copenhagen

8th April, 19___

Dr. Khayat
Gulf Union Incorporated
P.O. Box 233
Dubai
U.A.E.

Dear Dr. Khayat,

It was really most unfortunate that I was not in my office when you
called on me on 3rd April. Looking through our correspondence I see,
however, that we had fixed an appointment for 3 p.m. on 5th April,
and I had made myself available for you on that day. In fact I was hoping for the pleasure of your company during the evening as well.

I understand my secretary gave you some of the data you required since
you had to leave for Damascus next morning. Do let me know when
you expect to be in Copenhagen again, as I would very much like to
have an opportunity to talk to you about various matters of mutual
interest.

Sincerely,

B S Johansson

P.S. Johansson

Questions on the Letter

1. Why was Dr. Khayat not expected?
2. How was Mr. Johansson's secretary able to help Dr. Khayat?

1. Appointments and Travel Arrangements

c) Travel arrangements to be made

BY AIR MAIL: EXPRESS DELIVERY HOTEL INTOURIST
Baku, USSR

14th March, 19___

Dear Miss Rushton,

Thank you for sending me the most important mail of the last two weeks. It reached me here on my arrival at Baku yesterday. My business talks in the Soviet Union have been quite successful so far, and I look forward to reporting on them when I am back at the office at the end of the month. For the time being I am sending you my brief notes, which I would ask you to type as a draft before my return.

As you know from my itinerary, from here I am travelling by rail to Tiflis and on to Istanbul, where I shall be from 20–22 March. As it is rather difficult for me to make travel arrangements from here, would you please make the following reservations for me, and wire a confirmation to me at the Oriental Hotel, Istanbul. Would you please book me on a flight to Marseilles on 22nd of March and then to Manchester on the 26th. If possible try to find a direct flight from Marseilles to Manchester.

Please make first class reservations. I shall buy all the necessary tickets on my way, but these bookings should be made in my name.

Regards to all at the office,
Sincerely,

George Hamilton
George Hamilton

Miss D. Rushton
Ackland International
P.O. Box 9751
Manchester
England

Questions on the Letter

1. Why does Mr. Hamilton need his secretary's help in making travel arrangements?
2. What three things does he ask her to do for him?

---

1. Appointments and Travel Arrangements

d) Travel arrangements made

ACKLAND INTERNATIONAL MANCHESTER 12738
MR. G. HAMILTON ORIENTAL HOTEL ISTANBUL 16 3 19__

BA 109 DEPART 17 00 22 MARCH STOP HOTEL AMBASSADOR
MARSEILLES SINGLE ROOM 22–26 MARCH STOP DIRECT FLIGHT FULL
STOP BA 42 DEPART 13 00 STOP CONNECTION HEATHROW BC 18 00
STOP ARRIVE MANCHESTER 18 40

RUSHTON

Questions

1. What flight does Mr. Hamilton travel on, and when does it leave?
2. Where will he stay in Marseilles?
3. Why can't he travel straight to Manchester from Marseilles?

Phrases

Appointments

You asked us to let you know when it would
be convenient to us to have your representative call.

We suggest 28th September as a date for
your representative's visit, but not before
3 o'clock.

Please inform us of the time of his visit.

You suggested coming to our offices at 14.30
on Tuesday, 8th May.

We feel that 11.00 would be more convenient, since our Mr. Freeman will be available
then.

Since your marketing manager is engaged at
that time, we suggest a meeting at 10 a.m. on
March 17th.

---

1. Appointments and Travel Arrangements

Would you please arrange for our Mr. Carstairs to be met at Istanbul airport. He arrives at 17.10 hours on flight BE 421 from London.

Could we see each other for about an hour on Monday afternoon at 3 o'clock?

This is to confirm the appointment we made to meet at your showrooms at 3 p.m. on Monday, 20th February.

I would very much like to talk to you about this project the next time you are in London.

Travel Arrangements

Is there a flight from Tokyo to New Delhi via Bangkok on 1st April in the late afternoon? I have an open ticket for this route.

If not, please notify me of the next possible direct flight.

It was only possible to make a reservation from Tokyo to Bangkok. Your name has been placed on the waiting list for the flight from Bangkok to Delhi. The airlines, flight numbers and checking-in times are as follows:

The enclosed brochures may help you to choose an attractive tour and hotel accommodation.

It would help us considerably if you would book the following hotel accommodation at a convenient location for the period of our conference:

In reply to your letter, we confirm that we have made the reservations requested at the Central Hotel.

Terms are . . . for a single room with shower, and . . . for a double room with bath, inclusive of breakfast, service charges and VAT.

1. Appointments and Travel Arrangements

On account of a trade fair which is being held here, there are practically no hotel rooms available. However, we could book private accommodation for you, or look for a hotel out of town.

Please advise immediately if you wish us to reserve alternative accommodation.

As this stage of my journey is taking longer than expected, I should like to cancel my reservation on flight XYZ 349 to Chicago and the hotel booking there from July 15—18.

If you wish to hire a self-drive or chauffeur-driven car, arrangements can be made at the airport for immediate availability.

Rental, mileage and insurance will cost . . . per day for 100 miles.

1. Appointments and Travel Arrangements

2. Invitations: Accepting and Declining

A formal *invitation*, usually in the form of a letter or printed card, is written in the third person, and replies also follow the same style. Other invitations are written less formally. Any written invitation should be answered in writing too, not by phone.

A distinction is made between a *formal invitation*, a *semi-formal invitation* and an *informal invitation*, and the correct form of reply to each is indicated.

a) A formal invitation

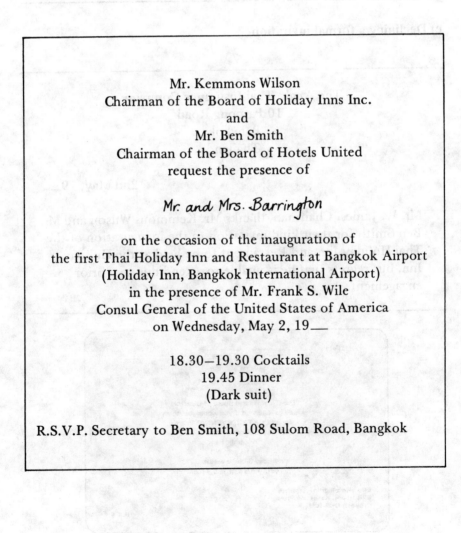

Mr. Kemmons Wilson
Chairman of the Board of Holiday Inns Inc.
and
Mr. Ben Smith
Chairman of the Board of Hotels United
request the presence of

Mr. and Mrs. Barrington

on the occasion of the inauguration of
the first Thai Holiday Inn and Restaurant at Bangkok Airport
(Holiday Inn, Bangkok International Airport)
in the presence of Mr. Frank S. Wile
Consul General of the United States of America
on Wednesday, May 2, 19____

18.30—19.30 Cocktails
19.45 Dinner
(Dark suit)

R.S.V.P. Secretary to Ben Smith, 108 Sulom Road, Bangkok

b) Accepting a formal invitation

> Hotel Cathay
> Bangkok
>
> 28th April, 19___
>
> Mr. and Mrs. J. Barrington thank Mr. Kemmons Wilson and Mr. Ben Smith for their kind invitation to the inauguration of the Thai Holiday Inn and Restaurant to be held at the Holiday Inn, and will be pleased to attend.

c) Declining a formal invitation

> The Anglo-Thai Insurance Company
> 10 Patpong Road
> Bangkok
> Thailand
>
> 2nd May, 19___
>
> Mr. W. James, Chairman, thanks Mr. Kemmons Wilson and Mr. Ben Smith for their kind invitation to the inauguration of the Thai Holiday Inn and Restaurant to be held at the Holiday Inn, but regrets that he is unable to attend due to a prior engagement.

ELLIS

The Chairman and Board of Directors
would be delighted if you would join them
for a COCKTAIL EVENING in the
Ballroom at the
'Inn on the Park'
Park Lane, W.1
on Friday 30th November 1973
between 6 p.m. and 9 p.m.

Ellis [Kensington] Limited,
Ellis House, Katharine Street,
Croydon CR9 1LN

R.S.V.P

2. Invitations

d) A semi-formal invitation

---

morgan stanley & co.
140 Broadway
New York, N. Y. 10005

August 17, 19___

Dear Dr. Trilling:

Mr. Mark A. Paul, Managing Director of Morgan & Cie International, and I are planning a small dinner party in honor of John D. de Butts, Chairman of the Board, and John J. Scanlon, Executive Vice President and Chief Financial Officer of the American Telephone and Telegraph Company. The dinner will be held at the Ambassador Hotel, Paris, beginning at 7:30 p.m. for 8:00 p.m. on Wednesday, September 12th, and dress will be informal business attire.

We hope that you will be able to join us in this opportunity to meet the senior management of the world's largest corporation. We look forward to seeing you on Wednesday, September 12th.

With warm regards,

Robert Baldwin

Robert H.B. Baldwin

Dr. Paul Trilling
The Bell Group
10–14 Beauchamp St.
London W1

Please reply: Mrs. Michèle Arnaud
Morgan & Cie International S. A.
4, Place de la Concorde
Paris 75008, France
Telephone: 266-03-19

---

2. Invitations

e) Declining a semi-formal invitation

the BELL group

10-14 Beauchamp Street London W 1

30th August, 19___

Dear Mrs. Arnaud,

Dr. Trilling, Chairman of the Bell Group, thanks you very much for the invitation to a dinner party at the Ambassador Hotel on 12th September, in honour of the senior management of the American Telephone and Telegraph Company.

He would be delighted to accept, but as he has already made arrangements to attend another important meeting which cannot be cancelled, Dr. Trilling unfortunately will not be able to attend the dinner.

Dr. Trilling has asked me to extend his cordial greetings to you, Mr. Paul, Mr. de Butts and Mr. Scanlon.

Yours sincerely,

Trilling.

Secretary to Dr. P. Trilling

f) Inviting a guest speaker

JOHN C. PATTERSON & SONS
Since 1868
Members of the New York Stock Exchange
103 Broadway
New York, N.Y. 10006

Mr. Stewart O'Neill
Chairman and President
Far East Telecommunications Corp.
P.O. Box 1090 Manila   June 17, 19__

Dear Mr. O'Neill:

As you may have heard, we regularly arrange meetings of our clients in
the States, in Europe, and in Asia, at which they have the opportunity
to listen to a talk held by leaders in commerce, or specialists in a field
of science.

Knowing of your vast experience in data processing and electronic communications, we are writing to ask you to be our guest speaker at a
luncheon to be held in Singapore on September 21. We would be very
pleased if you could give a talk of about one hour, and be kind enough
to answer questions afterwards. It would be useful if you could come
to the Hotel Continental at 11 a.m. to settle details of the program, or
if you could send us full particulars in writing beforehand.

Besides travelling expenses and two days' accommodation in Singapore,
we would pay you a fee of $400. We need hardly add that such a
meeting will serve to bring the operations of the Northern Telecommunications Corporation to the attention of an interested group of
businessmen.

We do hope you will be able to be present on this occasion.

                                             Sincerely yours,

                                             Paul Proctor

                                             Paul S. Proctor
                                             Senior Vice-President

PSP: nl

---

2. Invitations

1. Why are Patterson & Sons writing to Mr. O'Neill?
2. What do they offer him by way of compensation?

g) Invitation to lunch and a talk

JOHN C. PATTERSON & SONS
Since 1868
Members of the New York Stock Exchange
103 Broadway
New York, N.Y. 10006

Mr. H. Jackson
17 Orchard Road
Singapore

August 18, 19___

Dear Mr. Jackson,

On September 21 we are giving a luncheon for Mr. Stewart O'Neill, Chairman and President of Far East Telecommunications Corp. and Mr. Warren Morgan, Director of Investment Relations.

Mr. O'Neill will speak about the developments taking place in the dynamic areas of data processing and electronic communications, and Northern Telecommunications' role in these industries. Following lunch, our guests will be available to answer specific questions you may have. We think you will find this discussion interesting, and hope you can attend.

The luncheon will be held at the Hotel Europa, Scotts Road, Singapore at 12:00. Your prompt reply would be very much appreciated.

Sincerely yours,

Paul Proctor

Paul S. Proctor
Senior Vice-President

PSP: nl

Phrases

Invitations

The Chairman and Directors of the ...
Corporation have pleasure in inviting you to
attend a reception at (place) on (date) at
... p.m. in honour of (event).
R.S.V.P.

Dr. and Mrs. Eric Smythe request the pleasure of Mr. and Mrs. Daniel Wilkinson's
company at dinner on Saturday, 5th December at 7.30 p.m.

We hope that you will be able to join us at
this conference, and give us the benefit of
your experience.

Replies

Mr. and Mrs. Daniel Wilkinson thank Dr. and
Mrs. Eric Smythe for their kind invitation to
dinner, which they have much pleasure in
accepting.

Unfortunately I shall be out of town on
December 7th and will not, therefore, be
able to be present at the banquet you are
holding.

It will be a pleasure to see you again when I
visit New York next month.

I'm looking forward to becoming personally
acquainted with you after our long correspondence.

---

2. Invitations

3. Thanks for Hospitality, Requests, Complying with a Request

It is a matter of courtesy to write to your host personally if you have enjoyed his or her company's *hospitality*. Here you can see how to express *thanks* for the fulfilment of other *requests*, too.

a) Thanks for hospitality: request (business)

A Japanese insurance company writes to a Thai life insurance company

---

YASHIMA LIFE ASSURANCE COMPANY
Yo Tsui Chome
Tokyo

The Anglo-Thai Insurance Company   February 18, 19___
10 Patpong Road
Bangkok
Thailand

Gentlemen:

While I was in Thailand recently, I had the pleasure of visiting your company and hearing something of your business operations. I would like to thank you again for your very warm reception.

On reporting back to my managers in Tokyo, they showed great interest in the activities of your company. May I request you to send us a copy of your Annual Report and Accounts (in English, if possible) for last year, and to put the name of our company on the mailing list to receive your reports in future years.

Please accept our thanks in advance.

Sincerely yours,

T. Hakka

T. Hakka
Manager, Public Relations
YASHIMA LIFE ASSURANCE COMPANY

---

1. What line of business is Mr. Hakka engaged in and where?
2. What is his management interested in?
3. How can they follow the business activities of the Anglo-Thai Insurance Company regularly?
4. What is a mailing list?

b) Complying with a request

A Thai company sends a Japanese company its report and accounts

---

The Anglo-Thai Insurance Company

10 Patpong Road
Bangkok
Thailand

February 24, 19__

Mr. T. Hakka
Yashima Life Assurance Company
Yo Tsui Chome
Tokyo
Japan

Dear Mr. Hakka,

We also remember with pleasure the few days you spent with us, and the interesting talks we had.

Of course we shall be pleased to let you have a copy of our annual report regularly. However, the full report is printed in Thai only, though we issue a short version of the report and accounts in English.

I am enclosing a copy of each publication, and would be glad to hear from you which version you would like to receive in future years.

Sincerely yours,

John Dickson

Public Relations Dept.
Anglo-Thai Insurance Company

Enc.   Annual report and accounts (2)
          Short report (1)

---

3. Thanks

Questions on the Letter

1. Why can't the Anglo-Thai Insurance Company send a copy of the full Annual Report and Accounts in English?
2. What are they sending in the meantime?
3. What do they want to know from Mr. Hakka?

Phrases

Thanks

Thank you so much for your assistance/for the information you were able to give us.

It was most kind of you to give me the benefit of your experience.

Our exchange of ideas was most interesting.

We should like to express our sincere thanks for your valuable advice/for all the help you have given us.

I am most grateful to you for your warm hospitality during my recent stay in Singapore.

We should be happy to reciprocate your kindness at any time.

Please accept our warmest thanks.

Requests

I would be grateful if you could book hotel accommodation.

We would appreciate having the addresses of your branches abroad.

Please let me have full details.

I would like to receive this publication regularly.

3. Thanks

Kindly let us know as soon as possible what arrangements you have made.

Would you please let us have this information by next week.

I'm sure that I can count on your co-operation.

We would welcome any suggestions.

We should be most grateful for any help you can give us.

I trust you will give this request your kind consideration.

'Trust me, Mr Jackson—your affairs will receive my complete and undivided attention!'

3. Thanks

4. Employment: Applications, Letters of Recommendation, Giving Notice

When writing a letter of *application*, the applicant would like to say what job and conditions he or she would like to have. But a good letter of application should contain facts the prospective employer wants to know, for instance what experience the applicant has, how useful he will be to the company. If he has held several positions, it would be advisable for the applicant to submit a personal data sheet, our curriculum vitae, containing full personal details and information on past experience, education and certificates or degrees, special qualifications, and possibly references. The letter can then serve to draw the reader's attention to the candidate's suitability for the vacancy. If you are starting your career and have had one or two jobs, or none at all, all the particulars can be included in the letter itself.

A contract of employment defines the conditions of work, the working hours, holidays allowed, responsibilities and notice. It may contain a job description and give information on fringe benefits such as company pension scheme, bonuses, expenses and commission where applicable. When employment is terminated by either party, *notice* has to be given in writing and the set period observed.

'You're lucky. If you **had** been one of those clever, efficient young men who would have been able to take my place, I'd have got rid of you years ago!'

*Advertisement from a daily
newspaper offering a position
as salesman.*

Questions

1. What form of training will
   applicants undergo?
2. What fringe benefits can
   they expect?
3. What educational qualifications are required?
4. How and where will a meeting be arranged?

4. Employment

a) Application

17 Princes St.
Edinburgh
August 3, 1973

Sales Recruitment and Training Manager
W. & T. Avery Limited
21 Conduit St.
London W.1.

Dear Sirs,

In reply to your advertisement in today's 'Daily Telegraph', I am interested in becoming a salesman for your company.

As you can see from the enclosed curriculum vitae, I have selling experience in pharmaceuticals and cosmetics—a very competitive field. However, I would like to change to industrial products since I believe they offer a greater potential. Your six months' training scheme should certainly help me to devote the best of my ability to your company, particularly since my educational qualifications are higher than those you require.

My present position is subject to one month's notice, after which I would be able to train in London and, if necessary, relocate to any part of the country.

As you request in your advertisement, I shall telephone you shortly to make an appointment for a personal meeting. Meanwhile I thank you for considering my application.

Yours faithfully,

P. Ryder

Peter S. Ryder

Enc. Curriculum vitae

Curriculum Vitae

Peter S. Ryder

Personal details

Date of birth: February 2, 1951   Address: 17 Princes St.
                                                      Edinburgh

Marital status: Single   Phone: -021-765-1626

Education

Dundee University   Honours Degree:
                                          Chemistry
                                          III class

Business experience

1972–1976 Sales assistant with   Newton Pharmaceuticals Ltd.
                                          Windmill Estate
                                          Solihull
                                          Birmingham.

Special qualifications

Have attended an evening course in Marketing at R.S.A., intermediate
level, and shall sit for this examination next month.

Questions on the Letter and Curriculum Vitae

1. Why does Peter Ryder want to change jobs?
2. In what way are his educational qualifications higher than required?
3. What relevant training and experience has he had?
4. How soon would he be able to start employment with Avery?

'. . . and this is the staff canteen.'

---

4. Employment

b) Confirming employment

W.&T. Avery Limited

21 Conduit St.   London W.1.

August 15, 19___

Dear Mr. Ryder,

With reference to our telephone conversation of Friday, August 10, I am pleased to confirm the offer of a position as salesman in this company.

Enclosed are two copies of the contract of employment. Would you please sign both copies and return them to this office. The other enclosure is given to all employees and provides information relating to the superannuation fund, staff canteen, sports and social club, other facilities and fringe benefits.

Should you have any queries about your conditions of employment, please do not hesitate to contact this office.

I look forward to seeing you on October 1, and hope that this will be the beginning of a long and mutually beneficial association.

Yours sincerely,

J. Brown

for W. & T. Avery Limited
Personnel Manager

Encs.

Mr. Peter S. Ryder
17 Princes St.
Edinburgh.

Questions on the Letter

1. How has or will Mr. Ryder let Avery know of his willingness to accept the position?
2. How are the conditions of employment explained?
3. What other information is enclosed with the letter?
4. How can Mr. Ryder clear up any questions he may have regarding the conditions of employment?
5. When will Mr. Ryder start his training?

---

4. Employment

c) Contract of employment

W.&T. Avery Limited
21 Conduit St.   London W.1.

GENERAL CONDITIONS OF EMPLOYMENT

1. Hours are from 9.00 a.m. to 5.30 p.m. Monday to Friday.

2. Overtime is not paid, but should employees be requested to work outside normal working hours, time off will be given in lieu.

3. Three weeks' annual holiday plus usual statutory holidays. Annual holidays to be arranged through head of department.

4. One month's notice is required by either party after three months' trial period. One week's notice is required during the trial period.

5. Membership of trade unions is encouraged by the company, but a final decision on this matter is left to the employee.

6. Any complaint should be made through the head of department.

REMUNERATION OF FIELD STAFF
(Salesmen, Maintenance Staff)

7. During the first six months of induction and training a salary of . . . per annum will be paid.

8. Subsequently a salary of . . . per annum will be paid, plus 10% commission on normal sales and 15% for all new customers. Service increments are payable after two years. Performance bonuses are awarded at the discretion of the sales management.

9. Car expenses of . . . are paid per week/per month/per annum, and are reviewed every two years.

_____   _____

W. & T. Avery Limited   Employee

_____ 19__   _____ 19__

4. Employment

Questions on the Contract

1. What would happen if Mr. Ryder worked until 7.30 p.m. twice in a month?
2. What are statutory holidays?
3. How much notice would Mr. Ryder have to give if he wanted to leave the company after the trial period was over?
4. What is the company's attitude to their employees joining a trade union?
5. To whom should one complain if working conditions are unsatisfactory?

d) Giving notice

17 Princes St.
Edinburgh

August 26, 19___

REGISTERED MAIL

The Personnel Manager
Newton Pharmaceuticals Ltd.
Solihull
Birmingham

Dear Sir,

According to the terms of my employment contract, I hereby give one month's notice that I wish to terminate my employment with the company on September 30, 19___.

Please be assured that no dissatisfaction with the company is involved. The reason for my leaving is that I would like to extend my professional activities to a wider field of industry. At the same time I very much appreciate the opportunities I have had at Newton to gain experience in marketing and sales. I shall remember my superiors, colleagues and my work here with pleasure.

Yours faithfully,

P. Ryder

Peter S. Ryder

Questions on the Letter

1. Why does Mr. Ryder have to give one month's notice?
2. Why does he want to leave the company?
3. Why does he send the letter by registered mail?

4. Employment

e) Letter of recommendation (Testimonial)

To whom it may concern

We hereby testify that Miss Marie Obregon has been employed in our export department for three years.

Miss Obregon joined our staff as a junior secretary on March 1, 19___. It has continuously been her aim to improve her professional ability. She took evening courses in secretarial practice and English and a year ago became private secretary to our export manager, frequently handling Spanish and English correspondence independently. She was responsible for arranging sales promotion meetings, and preparing reports and minutes.

Miss Obregon was willing and able to take on increased responsibility where necessary, often acting as an interpreter in our connexions with English-speaking people.

She is giving up her position to get married in May. In taking leave of Miss Obregon, our company gratefully recognizes the help given and offers a wholehearted recommendation.

Brintex International
Avenida Juarez 1022
Mexico 12, D.F.

March 20, 19___

Phrases

Applications

With reference to your advertisement in 'The Times' of Friday, January 4th, I would like to apply for the position of . . . in your company.

I recently heard from . . . that there is a vacancy in your accounts department.

Please refer to the enclosed curriculum vitae/ personal data sheet for further particulars.

I am used to working on my own.

---

4. Employment

I would like the opportunity to work on my own initiative and to take on a certain amount of responsibility.

During training for my present job I took courses in marketing and sales promotion.

In view of my qualifications, I would expect a salary of about . . ., with the usual fringe benefits.

I am at present earning . . . per annum, plus expenses.

I would prefer to discuss the question of salary at a personal meeting.

The company with which I am employed at present does not, I feel, offer me enough scope to develop my own ideas.

Since my present position offers little prospect for advancement, I should prefer to be employed in an expanding organization such as yours.

Acceptance/Refusal

Thank you for your letter of January 28, and the enclosed information relating to your company.

Thank you for offering me the post/position of . . . .

I have pleasure in accepting the position.

I should like to accept the post, and look forward to joining your firm/staff on January 1.

I look forward very much to commencing work on January 1.

I am unable to accept your offer/the post.

I regret to inform you that I cannot accept the position, since I have received another, more attractive offer.

I feel that my experience in this field would not be used to its full capacity in the position you offer. Therefore I must decline.

4. Employment

5. Goodwill Letters: Congratulations, Introductions, Condolence, Christmas and New Year Wishes

A *goodwill letter,* as its name implies, is not written to obtain an order, or to collect outstanding bills. It is intended to pay for itself in another way, by building up goodwill. It is difficult to measure its value, but if this could be done businessmen would probably write goodwill letters more often. They give both the writer and the recipient pleasure when the occasion arises to enclose a gift, to send good wishes, to express thanks or to remember an anniversary. Letters of introduction can also be a great help, both to a young person starting out in a particular field of business and to the established businessman wishing to expand his operations.

Goodwill letters let customers feel that they are in touch—in good times and bad—when business friends show sympathy, when they offer assistance, and when congratulations are due.

'Dear Sir ... with reference to your letter of January 30th ....'

---

a) Goodwill letter

Bonds Forwarding Company **BFC** 117 Harbour Road, Southampton

17 June, 19___

Mr. Starros Alexiou
Alexiou Shipping Co.
125 Omonia Square
Athens

Dear Mr. Alexiou,

Looking through our files yesterday, I realized that it is just ten years since we started business together. So I'm really glad to have the opportunity of saying 'Thank you' for your regular custom.

Your recommendations to other potential customers have also shown me that you appreciate the service we offer.

We are grateful, and look forward to continuing our long association.

Yours sincerely,

John Bonds

John Bonds
BONDS FORWARDING COMPANY

Questions on the Letter

1. How long have Bonds Forwarding Company and the Alexiou Shipping Company been doing business together?
2. What does Bonds Forwarding Company appreciate?
3. What do the Alexiou Shipping Company appreciate?

---

5. Goodwill Letters

b) Congratulations

10 Bond Street
London W.1.

5th October, 19____

Dear Charles,

I have just learned that you have been appointed Regional Manager for the Middle East. Looking back on your activities so far, I know that your enthusiasm and experience are the very qualities that are needed for this position. I wish you every success in managing the affairs of the branch.

My colleagues join me in sending you our warmest congratulations.

With kindest regards,
Yours,

R. Wetherby
Randal Wetherby

Mr. Charles Lyons
Ferdosi Square
Rafat Iyah Street 86
Teheran
Iran

Questions on the Letter

1. What does Mr. Wetherby congratulate Mr. Lyons on?
2. According to Mr. Wetherby, what qualities does Mr. Lyons possess which make him particularly suited to this position?
3. Who also send their congratulations?

---

5. Goodwill Letters

c) Introducing a business friend

The Anglo-Thai Insurance Company
10 Patpong Road
Bangkok
Thailand

June 16, 19___

Mr. T. Hakka
Yashima Life Assurance Company
Yo Tsui Chome
Tokyo, Japan

Dear Mr. Hakka,

A friend of mine, Mr. Smarnchit Kamthon, would very much like to meet you. He is a student of Economics at the Chulalongkorn University, Bangkok (School of Applied Economics and Business Studies), and plans to enter the insurance business in a few months' time. Meanwhile he is making a study trip to Japan, in order to contribute towards a book which is in preparation entitled 'Social Insurance Abroad'.

You were kind enough, when you were here, to offer me your assistance. I would very much appreciate it if you could find time to see Mr. Kamthon, or to give him an introduction to someone on your staff. Thank you.

Yours sincerely,

Paul Saxer
Paul Saxer
Public Relations Department
ANGLO-THAI INSURANCE

Questions on the Letter

1. Who is Mr. Kamthon?
2. What are his plans?
3. What is he doing in the meantime?
4. In what way does Mr. Saxer ask Mr. Hakka to help him?

---

5. *Goodwill Letters*

d) Asking for introductions

Hunters Ranch,
Paxton, Florida 32538

May 4, 19___

Dear Mr. Wembley:

My wife and I are coming to Delhi for a fairly long stay, as I have business there that will keep me several months. I know you have lived in Delhi for several years, and I wonder if you would kindly give us some introductions.

Since I shall be very occupied, my wife may feel lonely at times. If she knew one or two people whom she could visit now and again, it would be very pleasant for her.

I would be most grateful for your help. If there is anything I can do for you—either here in the States or when I am in Delhi—please do not hesitate to let me know.

Sincerely yours,

Harold Canning

Harold Canning

Mr. Clifford Wembley
c/o American Press Office
New Delhi, India

Questions on the Letter

1. Why is Mr. Canning writing to Mr. Wembley?
2. How could introductions help him?
3. What assistance does Mr. Canning offer Mr. Wembley?

5. Goodwill Letters

e) Condolence

CAMBRIDGE ARCHAEOLOGICAL MUSEUM

29 December, 19___

Dear Mr. de Vere,

I was deeply distressed to hear of the sudden death of Mr. Arthur Williams who served on your Museum Board for so long. His passing must mean a great loss to your institution and his associates. We, who knew him, have good cause to be grateful to him for his sound judgement and advice that he gave us unreservedly.

My staff join me in conveying our sincere sympathy to members of his family.

Yours sincerely,

Bernard Glover

Mr. Peter de Vere
Curator
Museum of Archaeology and Ethnology
Hill Square
Edinburgh

Questions on the Letter

1. What had been Mr. Williams' connexion with the Edinburgh Museum?
2. Why did Mr. Glover have reason to be grateful to him?
3. To whom do Mr. Glover and his staff offer their condolences?

f) Get-well wishes

ICB **Inter-City Bank**
Jakarta Branch

February 17, 19___

PT Bank Bantu Dagang
JL Pasar Pagi 99
Jakarta
Indonesia

Dear Mr. Sukarman,

When your secretary called this morning to tell me that you would
not be able to keep our appointment due to a sudden illness, I was
deeply concerned.

I sincerely trust the medical attention you have received is one
hundred per cent successful, that your progress continues to your
benefit and to the satisfaction of your medical advisers, and that
your stay is as comfortable as possible in a pleasant environment.

The few small business matters which we were going to discuss can
quite easily wait until you are back in your usual robust health, and
at your desk again.

In the meantime, please accept my very best wishes for a complete
and speedy recovery.

Cordially yours,

Arthur R. Thompson

Arthur R. Thompson
Branch Manager

Questions on the Letter

1. Why was Mr. Sukarman unable to keep his appointment with Mr. Thompson?
2. When can their business be settled?

---

5. Goodwill Letters

g) Seasonal wishes

International Office Equipment Inc.
P.O. Box 295 Nassau
Bahamas

December 19, 19___

Ladies and Gentlemen:

Near the close of another year, we would like to take this opportunity of thanking our friends and customers for their continued
confidence and patronage.

We send you and your families our best wishes for Christmas and a
very prosperous New Year.

Sincerely yours,

H Rafferty

H. Rafferty

Questions on the Letter

1. Who are the International Office Equipment Inc. writing to?
2. What do they thank them for?
3. What do they wish them?

Phrases

Goodwill

Welcome to Hillbourne. To help you to get to know your city better, we are sending you a map showing the principal thoroughfares and the location of our bank.

We greatly appreciate your comments about our airline and hope that you will continue to enjoy flying with us.

Congratulations

It was with great pleasure that we heard of your appointment as Chairman. Please accept our heartiest congratulations.

Please convey our best wishes and congratulations to Mr. Howe on his promotion.

Congratulations to you and your wife on the birth of your son.

We should like to send you our congratulations on the occasion of your company's fiftieth anniversary.

Introductions

I should like to introduce Mr. Terence Russel, a personal friend of mine, who wishes to make some business contacts in your area.

I would be grateful if you could give him some information on local conditions and prospects in your line of business.

This would be a great favour, which I should be pleased to return at any time.

---

5. Goodwill Letters

Condolences

May I offer you my sincere condolences. If there is anything I can do to help you, please do not hesitate to let me know.

We were most grieved to hear of Miss Joan Harvey's death.

With gratitude we recall her unfailing kindness.

The sudden and unexpected passing of Mr. Walter Baron has, I am sure, created a gap in your organization which cannot be filled easily.

We can fully appreciate how deeply you must feel his loss.

You have the deepest sympathy of everyone on our staff.

Get-well Wishes

I trust that you are feeling better, and send you my best wishes for a speedy recovery.

We were very glad to hear that you are making good progress.

Seasonal Wishes

Please accept our best wishes for Christmas and the New Year.

Our directors and staff join in thanking you for your custom in the past year, and wish you health and happiness in 19__ .

4. Telegrams, Telex Messages

For fast action a written communication may be sent to your correspondent within hours by telegraph or telex.

To save expense a *telegram* should be short, but it must always be clear. It is therefore worthwhile taking some trouble to draft your message, for example:

First draft:

> CALLED AWAY ON URGENT BUSINESS SO WILL NOT BE ABLE TO SEE
> YOU ON WEDNESDAY NOVEMBER 14 STOP WILL BE BACK A WEEK
> LATER STOP
> SORRY ABOUT INCONVENIENCE   MAXWELL

can be shortened by writing:

> URGENT BUSINESS NECESSITATES CHANGED APPOINTMENT FROM
> NOVEMBER 14 TO 21
> SORRY   MAXWELL

Many companies have a short telegraphic address or a telex number to save words in addressing the message. Those sending wires frequently use one of the recommended codes (Bentley, ABC). For general purposes normal language is used, omitting the shorter, less important words and making use of these abbreviations:

RETEL	referring to telegram/telex
RELET	referring to letter
MYTEL	my telegram/telex
URTEL	your telegram/telex
OURTEL	our telegram/telex
CFM	confirm please
OK	agree
OK?	do you agree?
RPT	repeat
SOONEST	as soon as possible
ETA	expected time of arrival
BIBI	bye-bye: instead of Yours faithfully, to show end of message

Signs such as % or 0/0, & or +, ′(feet or minutes), ″(inches or seconds) count as one letter. Abbreviations can also be used. Up to five letters count as one word:

B/E	bill of exchange
CIF	cost, insurance, freight
COD	cash on delivery
DOZ	dozen
NY	New York
10AM	10 a.m.

Fractions count as three letters, so

21½ (or 21 1/2) can be sent as one word
211½ (or 211 1/2) would count as two words.

Since teleprinting errors are often made in transmitting such messages, the use of words instead of numbers and signs is often preferred:

GRANTSON LONDON

URTEL 7 MAY QUOTE LOWEST PRICE FOURHUNDRED SWINGER DRESSES INCLUDING FIVEPERCENT TRADE DISCOUNT

MATWILS CHICAGO

Do not divide words at the end of a line. Write the sender's name on a separate line.

There are various ways of sending telegrams, and the rates are calculated according to the speed with which they are delivered (inquire at your post office, telephone company or telegraph office):

Urgent	(double rate)
ELT	European letter telegram
LT	Night letter telegram (overseas)
RP 22	reply paid for 22 words

Telex (Teleprinter Exchange) enables participants to correspond with about 400,000 telex connexions all over the world.

If used frequently, telex communications are cheaper than telegrams, because they are calculated according to time, not the number of words. By using a punched tape, the telex operator is able to transmit messages at a speed of 400 characters per minute.

For this reason economy of words is less important here than clarity. Telex messages are usually sent abroad, and language misinterpretations can easily occur if the message is not perfectly clear.

Telegrams and telexes are not regarded as being legally binding, as they do not bear a signature. So important messages, especially orders, price changes, or any matter involving the writer in a commitment, should be confirmed by letter, which is signed for the company by the person responsible.

ACCOUNT LONG OVERDUE STOP URGE YOU REMIT $3700 BY JAN 10
TO AVOID EXPENSES OF LEGAL ACTION

Gentlemen: REGISTERED

As we received no reply to our repeated requests for payment of your account, we sent you the following telegram this morning:

ACCOUNT LONG OVERDUE STOP URGE YOU REMIT $3700 BY JAN 10
TO AVOID EXPENSES OF LEGAL ACTION

The amount of $3700 has been overdue since August 31, 19___, and since you have disregarded our reminders, we have no option but to place the matter in the hands of our lawyers.

You will certainly want to avoid the trouble and expense involved in a legal action so we request you urgently to settle your account by January 10.

                                     Very truly yours,

IV. Telegrams, Telex Messages

Phrases

Inquiries

request best price 2000 laboratory thermometers centigrade for delivery december

please wire if 2% cashdiscount margin included in price quoted

Quotations

thermometers required available mid-january only quotation mailed

magnet skiboots now reduced tenpercent special offer until end august subject goods unsold

Orders

please supply 2000 thermometers air-freight urlet 12 october order follows

require following spareparts for triumph 1300. 17/3bl quantity 20 18/2x8 quantity 81 72/51d quantity 200 soonest cfm

Delivery

approve prices notify exact dispatch date our order 394

your order x12 airfreighted today shipping documents airmailed

Complaints

artsilk received yesterday your invoice 1320. inferior to samples received 2 june suggest 25% price reduction or return consignment carforward

artsilk incorrectly addressed please return carforward. your material and rectified invoice dispatched today sorry

regret delay goods held up customs awaiting
certificate origin

Payments

invoice 2489 october 31 long overdue request
remittance soonest

regret delayed payment due to business difficulties request postponement. 40 dollars
now remainder 260 march

agree postponement will draw 60 days draft
for 260 plus 8% interest

Meetings

urgently request your presence at norwich
for special management committee meeting
planned 10 or 11 november cfm best date

away 10/11 november could attend 13
november please submit agenda express

agenda mailed meeting called 13 november
thanks

IV. Telegrams, Telex Messages

Exercises

SECTION II LETTERS ON BUSINESS SITUATIONS

1. Inquiries (p.11)

1. Why is the following letter unsatisfactory?

> Dear Sir,
>
> We recently saw an advertisement of yours for hooks. Please send us a quotation immediately.
>
>   Yours faithfully,

2. Write a letter from the following notes:

> Guazelli Company of Sao Paulo write on 3rd August 19___ to Taylor & Co., Mincing Lane, London EC4 asking for a special offer of Darjeeling tea. They will require at least 200 cases monthly, and would like prices, terms, delivery dates.

2. Quotations, Offers (p. 18)

1. Letter writing

Write a reply to your inquiry for hooks (above) quoting price, terms of payment and delivery date, and enclosing samples and an order form.

2. Write a letter from the following notes:

> Taylor & Co., London EC4 thank Guazelli Company, Sao Paulo (10th August 19___) for inquiry of August 3rd. In accordance with the request from Guazelli Company, they enclose their latest price list and samples. Their terms of payment are: cash against invoice. Should further orders follow, they are willing to allow Guazelli Company three months' credit. They look forward to a trial order.

3. Sales Letters, Changes in Business (p. 26)

1. Letter writing

You work for Jones and Co., who for the last five years have been the agents in your country for the products of Nippon Photoelectric, P.O. Box 362,

Tokyo. During this time your company has sold large numbers of the 'Superfax A5' copying machine. The latest sales figures however show a sudden fall and Photoelectric wrote one month ago to ask the reason why. Your Sales Manager has drafted a reply and wants you to write the letter. Write a business letter based on his instructions:

(a) Acknowledge letter.
(b) Apologize for delay. Give reason, e.g. absence from office.
(c) Fall in sales. Very worrying.
(d) Mention sales effort.
(e) Mention possible causes, e.g. recent price increase, competition.
(f) Refer to defects in machines.
(g) Give our opinion—new products needed.
(h) State need for effective measures.
(i) Willingness to give further details.
(j) Request comments.

2. Write a letter:

The Continental Sports Company Ltd. announces the opening of a new factory in Springvale, Scotland to produce skis made of glass fibre reinforced with plastic—special polyester provides elasticity and strength—originally planned to make ski poles of plastic too—instead collaboration arranged with the British Light Alloy Company of Brixton—ski poles manufactured of special light metal conical tube—skis and poles being offered at special introductory prices—price list enclosed.

4. Counter-Proposals, Concessions (p. 30)

1. Write a letter:

Guazelli Company of Sao Paulo write to Taylor & Co. on 17th August, pointing out that there is increased competition from new areas of tea production in Africa. The quality of the tea that Taylor & Co. offer is higher, but so are their prices. They ask the suppliers for a price reduction of 20%, in order that Guazelli Company can make a special introductory offer. Once their customers have bought the tea and have tasted it, there will be a much better chance of selling it at regular prices.

5. Orders, Order Acknowledgements (p. 33)

1. Write an order:

On 29th August Guazelli Company, Sao Paulo, thank Taylor & Co. for price concession. They now order for immediate delivery 150 cases of Darjeeling tea, No. 412. They request a credit of three months and ask for an acknowledgement of the order.

2. Write an acknowledgement:

On 5th September Taylor & Co. write that they are very pleased to receive Guazelli Company's order for 150 cases of Darjeeling tea, No. 412. They will be able to execute the order by the end of the month. Since they have not yet done any business with Guazelli, terms for this first order are cash against invoice. They enclose a pro-forma invoice and await an early reply.

6. Dispatch, Packing, Transport (p. 42)

1. Write a letter giving delivery instructions:

On August 7, Shirhana & Sons, forwarding agents of Port Road, Madras, India, send the Victoria Cycle Works delivery instructions on behalf of Worldwide Dealers of Hong Kong. The 42 containers are to be addressed to Shirhana's Madras warehouse and marked according to specifications. Besides the usual commercial invoices, a consular invoice and certificate of origin are required.

2. Write a letter giving advice of dispatch:

Victoria Cycle Works write to Shirhana & Sons on 17th August informing them that the bicycles have been dispatched according to their delivery instructions. Enclosed are the documents they requested.

7. Payment and Reminders (p. 48)

1. Letter writing

   (a) As MBM Ltd. have experienced very slack trade recently and have not been able to dispose of the consignment, they write to Astor Distributors Inc., 120 Webster St., Oakland, California 94612, making a proposal for extended terms of credit.

   (b) The invoice which Taylor & Co., London EC4, sent to Guazelli Company was due to be paid by October 15th. On November 15 Taylor & Co. write to their customers asking them to settle the overdue account.

8. Complaints, Handling Complaints (p. 56)

1. Letter writing

   (a) Guazelli Company write on 18th December 19__ saying that they are in a very awkward position, since they have not yet received the shipment advised by letter of 28th November from Taylor & Co., London EC4. They request supplier to explain the non-delivery.

   (b) Taylor & Co. reply on 23rd December 19__. Their forwarding agents have now been instructed to forward the cases of tea to Sao Paulo as soon as possible. They apologize for the inconvenience caused by this delay.

SECTION III LETTERS ON SOCIAL SITUATIONS

1. Letter writing

(a) Fernando Suarez of Guazelli Company is planning a business trip to England. Taylor & Co. have kindly placed a car at his disposal. Mr. Suarez would like to pay the expenses involved in its use, and inquires what expenses are likely to arise for petrol, maintenance, liability and other insurance, or if he has to pay a certain amount for mileage. He expects to travel 200-300 miles per week.

(b) Mr. Frank Swann will be attending a business meeting of Interplan Inc. in Copenhagen on Thursday and Friday. He asks for recommendations on coach and train trips, because he would like to spend some time touring Denmark.

1. Letter writing

(a) Write an invitation to an event you would like someone to attend, and
(b) write an acceptance.

1. Letter writing

(a) Write a request from these notes:
Your English teacher has given you the name of the Paddington School of Language Studies, 170 Warrington Avenue, London WC2A XC3. Write, asking for a prospectus and details of school fees for a 2-month course next summer (give dates). Can the school arrange for you to live with a family during the course? Mention your age and interests. You would be willing to share a room with a student of another nationality. Express thanks.
(b) Thank the manager for the way you were received during a week's period of training at an English company working in your field of business. Tell him how you will profit from what you saw and learnt.

1. Letter writing

(a) Write or find an advertisement for a job you would like.
(b) Write a letter of application for the job.
(c) You have had an interview. Write a letter accepting the job offered.
(d) Decline an offer of employment made by the Security Insurance giving reasons.

2. Write a letter of resignation.

Base your letter on the following notes:
You have been working for Bensons Engineering Company in Leeds as a translator for the past two years. Since the work is rather monotonous and there is little chance of advancement, you feel that you should accept the offer of a job in Iran which you have just received. Address your letter to the personnel manager.

5. Goodwill Letters, Congratulations, Introductions, Condolence, Christmas and New Year Wishes (p. 89)

1. Letter writing

   (a) Write a letter congratulating a former colleague of yours on his appointment as sales manager.
   (b) Your manager, who has been taken ill, is in hospital. Send him a book as a present from you and your colleagues, with good wishes for recovery.

SECTION IV TELEGRAMS, TELEX MESSAGES

1. Letter and telegram writing (p. 99)

   (a) Can you save your firm money by reducing the number of words in this telegram? If so, reword it more briefly.

WE HAVE NOT RECEIVED YOUR ORDER ACKNOWLEDGEMENT OF ORDER DATED 21 APRIL FOR 50 PAIRS OF VOGUE SHOES STOP WE REQUIRE THESE NOT LATER THAN 14 JUNE STOP PLEASE CHECK THE ORDER AND TIME OF DELIVERY AND REPLY BY WIRE

   (b) Evans & Donaldson of Louisville, Kentucky 40201 send a telex to their suppliers, Continental Tooling Service, 19 West Fourth Street, Dayton, Ohio 45401 as follows:

   contooling 658 31029 1973–8.20
   shipment order 912 due yesterday unreceived stop
   will return goods if not delivered by august 28

   evdonson

   Evans & Donaldson confirm this telex by letter, stressing that the goods are urgently required for customers to whom delivery has been promised by September 3. Write the letter.

Abbreviations

Key to Pronunciation

Phonetic Symbol	Word	(Transcription)	Phonetic Symbol	Word	(Transcription)
ɑː	father	'fɑːðə*	ŋ	long	lɔŋ
æ	bad	bæd	ŋg	longer	'lɔŋgə*
ai	cry	krai	ɔ	hot	hɔt
au	how	hau	o	obey	ə'bei, ou'bei
b	back	bæk	ɔː	saw	sɔː
d	day	dei	ɔi	boy	bɔi
dʒ	page	peidʒ	ou	so, sew, sow	sou
ð	then	ðen	p	put	put
e	wet	wet	r	red	red
ɛə	hair	hɛə*	s	sit, this	sit, ðis
ei	day	dei	ʃ	show, wish	ʃou, wiʃ
ə:	bird	bə:d	t	tin, hit	tin, hit
ə	ago, ladder	ə'gou, 'lædə*	tʃ	church	tʃə:tʃ
f	full, physics	ful, 'fiziks	θ	thin	θin
g	get	get	u:	boot	bu:t
h	hot	hɔt	u	good, put	gud, put
i:	meet	mi:t	uə	sure	ʃuə*
i	sit	sit	v	very	'veri
iə	hear	hiə*	ʌ	cup	kʌp
j	yes	jes	w	wet	wet
k	cold, kill	kould, kil	z	zero, his	'ziərou, hiz
l	like, fill	laik, fil	ʒ	pleasure	'pleʒə*
m	make	meik			
n	not	nɔt			

Vowels weakly accented within a word are often omitted. Thus, the syllable -tion, which is transcribed in this wordist [-ʃən] , is usually [-ʃn] . So *adoption* may be either [ə'dɔpʃən] or [ə'dɔpʃn] .

The asterisk (*) is used to indicate possible r-linking. Thus the word *father* is transcribed ['fɑːðə*] . When a word beginning with a consonant sound follows, the pronunciation is ['fɑːðə] . When a word beginning with a vowel sound follows, the pronunciation is ['fɑːðər] , as in 'the father of these children' [ðə 'fɑːðər əv ðiːz 'tʃildrən] .

Abbreviations

a	adjective	pl	plural
adv	adverb	pred	predicate
Am	American	prp	preposition
Br	British	s	substantive
f	feminine	sing	singular
fam	colloquial	s.o.	someone
intr	intransitive	s.o.'s	someone's
m	masculine	s.th.	something
n	neuter	tr	transitive
o.'s	one's	v	verb

Reference Vocabulary

to abandon [ə'bændən]
  to abandon a claim
abroad [ə'brɔ:d]
accept [ək'sept]
acceptance [ək'septəns]
  to present a bill for acceptance
accommodation(s *pl*) [ə,kɔmə'deiʃən(z)]
  hotel accommodation
accordance (with) [ə'kɔ:dəns]
account [ə'kaunt]
  accounts pl
  bank account
  brief account
  checking account
  credit an account
  current account, account current
  as per account
  to open an account with a bank
  savings account
  settle one's account
accountancy [ə'kauntənsi]
accountant [ə'kauntənt]
  chartered accountant
accounting [ə'kauntiŋ]
  factory accounting
to accrue [ə'kru:]
  accrued interest
to acknowledge [ək'nɔlidʒ]
  to acknowledge receipt of a letter
acknowledgement [ək'nɔlidʒmənt]
  acknowledgement of a debt
act [ækt]
  by act of law
adding machine ['ædiŋ mə'ʃi:n]
addition [ə'diʃən]
address [ə'dres]
  envelope address
  inside address
  return address
  telegraphic address
addressee [,ædre'si:]
to adjust [ə'dʒʌst]
  to adjust accounts
  to adjust an entry
adjustment [ə'dʒʌstmənt]
administration [əd,minis'treiʃən]
admit [əd'mit]
advance [əd'va:ns]
  cash advance
  advance payment
  advance on salary
  to book in advance

advertising ['ædvətaiziŋ]
  direct advertising
  radio advertising
  television advertising
  advertising agency
advertisement [əd'və:tismənt]
advise [əd'vaiz]
  as per advice
  no advice
  credit advice
advisable [əd'vaizəbl]
advise [əd'vaiz]
adviser [əd'vaizə]
  legal adviser
  technical adviser
advisory [əd'vaizəri]
  in an advisory capacity
  advisory committee
  advisory opinion
to affect [ə'fekt]
  This did not affect the result.
agency ['eidʒənsi]
  head agency
  travel agency
agenda [ə'dʒendə]
  to adopt the agenda
  to be on the agenda
agent ['eidʒənt]
  forwarding agent
  insurance agent
  local agent
  sole agent
agreement [ə'gri:mənt]
  according to agreement
  by mutual agreement
  agreement in writing
  to come to an agreement
aid [eid]
  to administer first aid
  economic aid
aircraft ['ɛəkra:ft]
  aircraft industry
airline ['ɛəlain]
airliner ['ɛə,lainə]
air mail ['ɛə meil]
  by air mail
airport ['ɛəpɔ:t]
  The aircraft left London Airport this morning.
air terminal ['ɛə ,tə:minl]
air traffic ['ɛə ,træfik]
to allocate ['æləkeit]

to allocate shares
to allocate expenses
allocation [,ælə'keiʃən]
allocation of seats
allocation of shares
allowance [ə'lauəns]
expense allowance
family allowance
mileage allowance
daily/per diem allowance
tax allowance
travelling allowance
to alter ['ɔ:ltə]
to alter the arrangements
alternative [ɔ:l'tə:nətiv]
He has no other alternative.
alternatively [ɔ:l'tə:nətivli]
anniversary [æni'və:səri]
to analyse ['ænəlaiz]
analysis, *pl* **-ses** [ə'næləsis, -i:z]
in the last analysis
analysis of expenses
anchorage ['æŋkəridʒ]
anchorage-dues pl
to announce [ə'nauns]
to announce on the radio
announcement [ə'naunsmənt]
announcement of sale
announcer [ə'naunsə]
annual ['ænjuəl]
annual general meeting
annual report
to anticipate [æn'tisipeit]
to anticipate payment
The amount was larger than I had
anticipated.
to apologize [ə'polədʒaiz]
We apologize for the delay.
apology [ə'polədʒi]
Please accept our apologies.
apparent [ə'pærənt]
apparent damage
to appeal [ə'pi:l]
to appeal to a higher court
The article appeals to the customers.
appliance [ə'plaiəns]
applicable [æplikəbl]
applicant ['æplikənt]
applicant for a job
application (form) [,æpli'keiʃən fɔ:m]
to appreciate [ə'pri:ʃieit]
I would appreciate it, if . . . .
He appreciates the fact that the work
cannot be done immediately.
appreciation [ə,pri:ʃi'eiʃən]
to show an appreciation
He does not expect any appreciation.
approach [ə'proutʃ]
approach to a subject
He is using the right approach.

appropriate [ə'proupriit]
if appropriate
at the appropriate time
approval [ə'pru:vəl]
on approval
His remark met with great approval.
approximate [ə'proksimit]
approximate value
approximately three months
area ['ɛəriə]
parking area
shopping area
trading area
area code Am
arise [ə'raiz]
aspect ['æspekt]
They studied every aspect of the
question.
to assemble [ə'sembl]
to assemble data
They assembled in the hall.
to assemble an engine
assembly [ə'sembli]
assembly hall
assembly line
assembly plant
assent [ə'sent]
He gave his assent.
to assert [ə'sə:t]
to assert a claim
to assess [ə'ses]
to assess the amount of damage
assets *pl* ['æsets]
fixed assets
assets and liabilities
to assist [ə'sist]
assistance [ə'sistəns]
Can I be of any assistance to you?
national assistance
assistant [ə'sistənt]
shop assistant
assistant manager
associate [ə'souʃieit]
to assume [ə'sju:m]
Let us assume that . . . .
He assumed new duties.
assumption [ə'sʌmpʃən]
on the assumption that . . .
assurance [ə'ʃuərəns]
He gave me his assurance that he would
be here.
to assure [ə'ʃuə]
attendance [ə'tendəns]
We had a good attendance at the meeting.
attention [ə'tenʃən]
attention: Mr. John Heely
for your kind attention
for immediate attention
to draw attention to
attitude ['ætitju:d]

You have the wrong attitude towards
  your work.
He adopted a negative attitude.
auction ['ɔːkʃən]
  to sell by (Am at) auction
audit ['ɔːdit]
  to make an audit
  annual audit
auditor ['ɔːditə]
authority [ɔːˈθɔriti]
  He has full authority to act.
  by authority
  the authorities pl
to authorize ['ɔːθəraiz]
  to be authorized to sign
  through authorized channels
automatic [ˌɔːtəˈmætik]
automation [ˌɔːtəˈmeiʃən]
availability [əˈveiləˈbiliti]
aviation [ˌeiviˈeiʃən]
  civil aviation
award [əˈwɔːd]
awkward ['ɔːkwəd]

background ['bækgraund]
  He stayed in the background.
  He has a very good background.
  educational background
  financial background
backing ['bækiŋ]
  currency backing
backlog ['bæklɔg]
  backlog of orders
  backlog demand
balance ['bæləns]
  to strike a balance
  balance brought forward
  balance at the bank
  balance on/in hand
  balance of payments
  balance of trade
  balance sheet
to balance ['bæləns]
  to balance our account
  to balance the books
bale [beil]
bank [bæŋk]
  bank of issue
  savings bank
  bank account
  bank discount
  bank note
  bank rate
  bank transfer
banker ['bæŋkə]
banking ['bæŋkiŋ]
  banking account
  banking hours pl
bankrupt ['bæŋkrʌpt]

to go bankrupt
bankruptcy ['bæŋkrəp(t)si]
to bargain ['baːgin]
  We had to bargain for everything.
  collective bargaining
  bargaining point
  bargaining position/power
to base on [beis]
  His statements are based on facts.
basic ['beisik]
  basic fact
  basic industry
  basic requirements pl
  basic training
  basically
basis, pl -ses ['beisis, -iːz]
  on the basis of facts
  to form/to lay the basis of s.th.
  basis of discussion
bearer ['bɛərə]
  payable to bearer
  cheque to bearer
behalf [biˈhaːf]
  on behalf of
benefit ['benifit]
  for the benefit of a third party
  fringe benefit
  social/insurance benefit
  sickness benefit
  unemployment benefit
bid [bid]
  highest/lowest bid
  call for bids
to bid (bid, bid[den]) [bid]
  He bid a fair price.
bidder ['bidə]
  highest bidder
  no bidders
bill [bil]
  air way bill
  bill of exchange
  bills payable
  bill of lading
  bill of health
  He paid the bill.
board [bɔːd]
  board meeting
  board of directors
  Board of Trade
  on board (a) ship
bond [bɔnd]
  in bond
  investment bonds pl
  bonded warehouse
bonus ['bounəs]
  cost-of-living bonus
  incentive bonus
  performance bonus
to book [buk]
  all booked up

He booked in advance.
to book an order
to book a room
to book a ticket
booking ['bukiŋ]
book-keeper ['buk,ki:pə]
book-keeping ['buk,ki:piŋ]
boom [bu:m]
building boom
to boost [bu:st]
to boost business
to boost prices
borrower ['bɔrouə]
borrowing ['bɔrouiŋ]
borrowing power
boss [bɔs]
to boss s.o. around
boundary ['baundəri]
boycott ['bɔikɔt]
bracket ['brækit]
salary bracket
branch office ['bra:ntʃ,ɔfis]
branch manager
brand [brænd]
What brand does he smoke?
brand name
branded goods pl
breakage ['breikidʒ]
breakdown ['breikdaun]
breakdown of costs/cost breakdown
breakdown of/in negotiations
brief [bri:f]
in brief
Please be brief.
briefing
briefcase ['bri:fkeis]
brisk [brisk]
brisk demand
to sell briskly
Business is brisk.
brochure [bro'ʃjuə]
broker ['broukə]
brought forward [brɔ:t 'fɔ:wəd]
budget ['bʌdʒit]
to draw up a budget
family budget
budget-priced
building trade ['bildiŋ treid]
bulk [bʌlk]
to sell in bulk
bulk article
bulk buying
bulky goods pl ['bʌlki gudz]
bulletin ['bulitin]
news bulletin
bulletin board
buyer ['bai-ə]
buyer's market/strike
chief buyer
by-product ['bai,prɔdʌkt]

cable ['keibl]
by cable
cable address
cable order
to calculate ['kælkjuleit]
They calculated the costs.
calculation [,kælkju'leiʃən]
according to my calculation
I am out in my calculation.
rough calculation
calculation of profits
call [kɔ:l]
at/on call
to be called for
money at call/call money
long-distance/trunk call
reversed charge call, Am *collect call*
call box
I called on him at his office.
to call at a port
caller ['kɔ:lə]
calling ['kɔ:liŋ]
calling on customers
calling card
campaign [kæm'pein]
advertising campaign
sales campaign
to cancel ['kænsəl]
until cancelled
They cancelled the order.
The meeting/The appointment was
cancelled.
cancellation [,kænsə'leiʃən]
cancellation of an entry
cancellation of a postage stamp
capacity [kə'pæsiti]
in a managerial capacity
working to capacity
seating capacity of a room
in his capacity as a chairman
capital ['kæpitl]
invested capital
working capital
capital goods pl
capital market
carbon copy ['ka:bən 'kɔpi]
carbon paper ['ka:bən 'peipə]
card-index ['ka:d,indeks]
career [kə'riə]
to enter upon a career
career woman
cargo, pl **-oes** ['ka:gou, -z]
mixed cargo
to discharge a cargo
carriage ['kæridʒ]
by land carriage
carriage-free/-paid
carriage forward
carriage by rail/by sea
carrier ['kæriə]

to carry forward [ˈkæri ˈfɔːwəd]
   to carry forward to new account
carrying [ˈkæriiŋ]
   carrying agent
   carrying business
   carrying trade
cash [kæʃ]
   for ready cash
   cash in hand
   cash on delivery (C.O.D.)
   cash account
   cash discount
   to cash a cheque
   He is out of cash.
cashier [kæˈʃiə]
   to pay the cashier
catalogue, *Am* **catalog** [ˈkætəlɔg]
   price catalogue
   catalogue price
category [ˈkætigəri]
to cater (for) [ˈkeitə]
   catering industry
   to cater to popular taste
caution [ˈkɔːʃən]
   Caution! Men at work!
ceiling [ˈsiːliŋ]
central [ˈsentrəl]
   central bank
certificate [səˈtifikit]
   certificate of origin
   to produce a certificate
to certificate [səˈtifikeit]
to certify [ˈsəːtifai]
   This is to certify that . . . .
chain [tʃein]
   chain store
chairman [ˈtʃɛəmən]
channel [ˈtʃænl]
   through official channels
   channels pl of supply
charge [tʃɑːdʒ]
   free of charge
   There is no charge.
   He charged him too much.
   Who is in charge of this office?
chart [tʃɑːt]
   weather chart
   organization chart
charter [ˈtʃɑːtə]
   charter plane
   chartered accountant
check [tʃek]
   luggage check
   coat/hat check
   checkpoint
   checkroom
   to check in/out
   to check baggage
cheque, *Am* **check** [tʃek]
   to draw/to endorse a cheque

to present a cheque for payment
honour a cheque
cheque book
stop a cheque
cheque to bearer
crossed cheque
open cheque
postal cheque
traveller's cheque
cheque card
choice [tʃɔis]
circular [ˈsəːkjulə]
   c.i.f. (cost, insurance, freight)
   circular letter of credit
   circular ticket/tour
to circulate [ˈsəːkjuleit]
circulation [ˌsəːkjuˈleiʃən]
   monetary circulation
   The magazine has a wide circulation.
circumstance [ˈsəːkəmstəns]
   in/under these circumstances
   under no circumstances
claim [kleim]
   to put in a claim
   *The insurance company paid all the
      claims against us.*
   He claimed damages.
clarity [ˈklæriti]
classification [ˌklæsifiˈkeiʃən]
class [klɑːs]
   cabin class
   economy class
to classify [ˈklæsifai]
   classified advertisements pl
   classified directory
clear [kliə]
   to clear a bill
   *He cleared his luggage at the
      customs.*
   clear profit/loss
clearance [ˈkliərəns]
   clearance sale
clearing [ˈkliəriŋ]
   clearing-house
clerical [ˈklerikəl]
   clerical error
   clerical work
client [ˈklaiənt]
c/o (care of)
c.o.d. (cash on delivery)
code [koud]
   highway code
   post/Am zip code
   code number
collaboration [kəˌlæbəˈreiʃən]
   in collaboration with
to collect [kəˈlekt]
   to collect outstanding debts
   to collect taxes
   to collect the luggage

to collect the letters
collect call Am, Br *reversed charge call*
collection [kə'lekʃən]
collection agency
collection department
collection of samples
column ['kɔləm]
in the second column on the first page
combination [ˌkɔmbi'neiʃən]
combine ['kɔmbain]
combine price
to combine [kəm'bain]
commercial [kə'mə:ʃəl]
commercial aviation
commercial correspondence
commercial television
commercial traveller
commission [kə'miʃən]
on a commission basis
He is a member of the commission.
The goods are sold on commission.
commission agent
commitment [kə'mitmənt]
without any commitments
committee [kə'miti]
to appoint a committee
ad hoc committee
advisory committee
joint committee
standing committee
steering committee
commodities pl [kə'mɔditiz]
to communicate (with) [kə'mju:nikeit]
communication [kəˌmju:ni'keiʃən]
Communications had been cut.
He is in communication with us.
a means of communication
company ['kʌmpəni]
joint stock company
company meeting
company property
comparison [kəm'pærisən]
to make a comparison
comparison of costs
to compensate (for) ['kɔmpenseit]
compensation [ˌkɔmpen'seiʃən]
We had to pay compensation.
as/by way of compensation
compensation claim
to compete with [kəm'pi:t]
competent ['kɔmpitənt]
competition [ˌkɔmpi'tiʃən]
to enter into competition with
They are in competition with each other.
free/unfair competition
competitive [kəm'petitiv]
competitive field
on a competitive basis
under fully competitive conditions
competitive price

competitor [kɔm'petitə]
complaint [kəm'pleint]
cause for complaint
letter of complaint
completion [kəm'pli:ʃən]
near completion
completion date
compliance [kəm'plaiəns]
in compliance with your instructions
to complicate ['kɔmplikeit]
complimentary [kɔmpli'mentəri]
complimentary close
to comply with [kəm'plai]
They complied with his instructions.
to comply with a request/a wish
to comply with the terms
component (part) [kəm'pounənt]
comprehensive [ˌkɔmpri'hensiv]
comprise [kəm'praiz]
compulsory [kəm'pʌlsəri]
computer [kəm'pju:tə]
to computerize [kəm'pju:təraiz]
concerned [kən'sə:nd]
all parties concerned
concerning [kən'sə:niŋ]
concession [kən'seʃən]
to make no concessions
to conclude (from) [kən'klu:d]
What do you conclude from his letter?
to conclude an agreement/a contract
conclusion [kən'klu:ʒən]
He has come to the same conclusion.
at the conclusion of his speech
to draw a conclusion
conclusion of an agreement
conditional acceptance [kən'diʃnl
ək'septəns]
condolence [kən'douləns]
to conduct [kən'dʌkt]
to conduct a business
to conduct negotiations
conducted tour
conference ['kɔnfərəns]
at the conference
He took part in a conference.
to preside at a conference
conference room/table
confidential [ˌkɔnfi'denʃəl]
private and confidential
to confirm [kən'fə:m]
to confirm an order/a report
confirmation [ˌkɔnfə'meiʃən]
congratulations [kən'grætjuleiʃənz]
connection [kə'nekʃən]
in this connection
in connection with
He missed his connection.
business connections pl
consent [kən'sent]
by common consent

consideration [kən'sidə'reiʃən]
he took into consideration
considering [kən'sidəriŋ]
consign [kən'sain]
consignee [ˌkɔnsai'ni:]
consignment [kən'sainmənt]
on consignment
consignment note
consignor [kən'sainə]
to consult [kən'sʌlt]
to consult a dictionary
consultant [kən'sʌltənt]
marketing consultant
firm of consultants
consumer [kən'sju:mə]
consumer goods pl
consumer industry
consumer resistance
consumption [kən'sʌmpʃən]
power consumption
contact ['kɔntækt]
to contact [kən'tækt]
You can contact me by phone.
container [kən'teinə]
contend [kən'tend]
to contend with a problem
contract ['kɔntrækt]
by contract
to make/to enter into a contract
contractor [kən'træktə]
building contractor
to contribute [kən'tribjú(:)t]
contribution [ˌkɔntri'bju:ʃən]
to make a contribution
employer's contribution
control [kən'trəul]
control of purchasing power
price control
controlled prices pl
controller [kən'trəulə]
convenience [kən'vi:njəns]
at your earliest convenience
all modern conveniences
convenient [kən'vi:njənt]
It is not convenient for me to come just now.
conversion [kən'və:ʃən]
conversion of a plant to . . . .
conversion table
conversion loan
to convert [kən'və:t]
to convert into cash
to cooperate [kou'ɔpəreit]
cooperation [kou,ɔpə'reiʃən]
cooperative (society) [kou'ɔpərətiv sə'saiəti]
(consumer) cooperative
cooperative bank
to co-ordinate [kou'ɔ:dineit]
to cope with [koup]
He had to cope with the situation.

copy ['kɔpi]
certified copy
corporation [ˌkɔ:pə'reiʃən]
public corporation
corporation tax
correspondence [ˌkɔris'pɔndəns]
I take care of/I handle the correspondence.
correspondence clerk
correspondent [kɔris'pɔndənt]
cost [kɔst]
cost of living allowance
cost of living index
cost free
at cost price
cost of production
counter ['kauntə]
to sell over the counter
counter proposal
to countermand [ˌkauntə'mɑ:nd]
coupon ['ku:pɔn]
dividend coupon
courtesy ['kə:təsi]
cover ['kʌvə]
under separate cover
coverage ['kʌvəridʒ]
full coverage
credit ['kredit]
credit standing
extension of credit
credit an amount to an account
credit and debit
on credit
sale on credit
three months credit
credit with a savings bank
to grant/to open a credit
to the credit of your account
credit balance
credit note
creditor ['kreditə]
crisis, *pl* -es ['kraisis, -i:z]
economic/financial crisis
currency ['kʌrənsi]
currency control/reform
foreign currency
current ['kʌrənt]
at the current rate of exchange
current account
current price
current events pl
custom ['kʌstəm]
according to custom
This shop has little custom.
customer ['kʌstəmə]
chance/regular customer
long-standing customer
customs ['kʌstəmz]
to pay customs duty
The passengers went through the customs.

customs clearance
customs officer
cut (cut, cut) [kʌt]
to cut prices
to cut rates
He has cut his losses.
price cut, cut in prices
cut in salary

damage ['dæmidʒ]
He had to pay damages.
to do damage
action for damages
to sue for damages
to claim damages
seriously damaged
data pl [deitə]
personal data
data processing
date [deit]
at an early date
date as per postmark
date of maturity
date of invoice
delivery date
day [dei]
eight-hour day
per day
pay day
dead [ded]
dead market
dead weight
dead season
deadline ['dedlain]
He met the deadline.
He is always working to a deadline.
deadlock ['dedlɔk]
deal (with) [di:l]
It's a deal!
square deal
He made a lot of money on that deal.
He deals in textiles.
Can you deal with . . .?
They closed the deal.
dealer ['di:lə]
wholesale dealer
used-car dealer
dealing ['di:liŋ]
cash deal
dealing in real estate
to have dealings with s.o.
debit ['debit]
to the debit of
your debit balance
to debit an account
on the debit side
debtor ['detə]
debts pl [dets]
bad debts

He is in debt.
decimal ['desiməl]
decline [di'klain]
decline in business
decline of/in prices
decline in production
decline in sales
He declined their offer.
declining sales pl
decrease ['di:kri:s]
decrease in population/in prices
decrease in value
to be on the decrease
to decrease [di:'kri:s]
Oil consumption has decreased.
to deduct from [di'dʌkt]
Deduct ten per cent.
deduction [di'dʌkʃən]
after deduction of expenses
defect [di'fekt]
defective [di'fektiv]
deficit ['defisit]
to show a deficit
definite ['definit]
definite booking
definite order
They came to a definite understanding.
delay [di'lei]
delivered [di'livəd]
delivered free
delivery [di'livəri]
delivery date
delivery instructions
payable on delivery
delivery of letters
delivery note
delivery times
demand (for) [di'ma:nd]
to be very much in demand
supply and demand
payable on demand
to demonstrate ['demənstreit]
He'll demonstrate how the machine works.
demonstration [,deməns'treiʃən]
to give a demonstration
demonstration model
department [di'pa:tmənt]
accounts/export department
head of department
sales department
service department
department store
departure (for) [di'pa:tʃə]
deposit [di'pɔzit]
to make a deposit at the bank
to pay/to leave a deposit
He deposited his money in the bank.
deposit account
deposit slip
depreciation [di,pri:ʃi'eiʃən]

depression [di'preʃən]
  economic depression
  market depression
design [di'zain]
  our latest designs
  registered design
designer [di'zainə]
desk [desk]
  Pay at the cash-desk.
  reception desk
destination [,desti'neiʃən]
  He reached his destination.
details ['di:teils]
  full details
  further details
devaluation [,di:vælju'eiʃən]
to devalue ['di:'vælju:]
development [di'veləpmənt]
device [di'vais]
  safety device
to dial ['daiəl]
  He dialled the wrong number.
  dialling tone
  dialling code
to diminish [di'miniʃ]
disadvantage [,disəd'va:ntidʒ]
  I'm at a disadvantage.
discount ['diskaunt]
  less discount
  to raise/to lower the discount
  cash discount
  cash without discount
  group discount
  special discount
  trade discount
discrepancy [dis'krepənsi]
discretion [dis'kreʃən]
to dismantle [dis'mæntl]
dispatch [dis'pætʃ]
  dispatch department
  ready for dispatch
  dispatch note
display [dis'plei]
  window display
  The goods are on display.
disposal [dis'pouzl]
  for disposal
  He/It is at your disposal.
to dispose of [dis'pouz]
  He disposed of his business.
  We had to dispose of our house.
to dissolve [di'zɔlv]
distribute [dis'tribju:t]
distribution [,distri'bju:ʃən]
  distribution of dividends
  distribution of a film
distributor [dis'tribjutə]
dividend ['dividend]
  dividend warrant
dock [dɔk]

dry/floating dock
document ['dɔkjumənt]
documentary [,dɔkju'mentəri]
  documentary credit
domestic [də'mestik]
  domestic market
  domestic production
down [daun]
  down payment
draft [dra:ft]
  draft payable at sight
  He made a draft on the firm.
  final draft
draw (on) [drɔ:]
  to draw a bill of exchange on s.o.
  to draw a cheque/Am check
  to draw money from an account
drawback ['drɔ:bæk]
drive [draiv]
  sales drive
drive-in [draiv-in]
drop [drɔp]
  drop in prices/turnover
  drop in production
due [dju:]
  in due course
  The rent is due next month.
  They are due to return today.
  due date
dues pl [dju:z]
  membership dues
duly ['dju:li]
  The letter is duly signed.
duplicate ['dju:plikit]
  in duplicate
  to make out in duplicate
to duplicate ['dju:plikeit]
duty ['dju:ti]
  liable to duty
  duty-paid
  customs duties pl
  duty-free shop

earnings pl ['ə:niŋz]
  annual earnings
  hourly earnings
economic [,i:kə'nɔmik]
  economic conditions pl
  economic development
  economic recovery
economical [,i:kə'nɔmikəl]
economy [i(:)'kɔnəmi]
  free economy
  planned economy
  economy class
  economy fare
education [,edju(:)'keiʃən]
  general education
  professional education

educational [ˌedju(ː)'keiʃənl]
educational film
effect (on) [i'fekt]
to go/to come into effect, to take effect
This event had an adverse effect on the
market.
with effect from
to effect payment
a phone call to the same effect
effective [i'fektiv]
effective from/as of January 1st
effective immediately
to become effective
effective measures pl
efficiency [i'fiʃənsi]
efficiency expert
efficiency bonus
efficient [i'fiʃənt]
He is very efficient in his work.
an elaborate scheme
electrician [ilek'triʃən]
electrification [iˌlektrifi'keiʃən]
electronic, *adv* -ally [ilek'trɔnik]
electronic brain
electronics [ilek'trɔniks]
element ['elimənt]
There is always an element of uncertainty
involved.
eligible ['elidʒəbl]
He is eligible.
to eliminate [i'limineit]
We had to eliminate all difficulties/the
causes.
elimination [iˌlimi'neiʃən]
to embark (for) [im'baːk]
to embark upon s.th.
He embarked upon a business career.
embarkation card [ˌemba'keiʃən kaːd]
emergency [i'məːdʒənsi]
in an emergency/in case of emergency
emergency door/exit
emergency landing
emigrant ['emigrənt]
to emigrate to ['emigreit]
emigration [ˌemigreiʃən]
employee [ˌemplɔi'iː]
employer [im'plɔiə]
employment [im'plɔimənt]
The factory provides employment for
many men.
employment agency
conditions of employment
employment market
to enable [i'neibl]
This enabled him to find a good job.
to enclose [in'klouz]
Enclosed please find . . . .
He enclosed a photograph with his letter.
enclosure [in'klouʒə]
to encroach [in'kroutʃ]

That's encroaching upon his rights.
to endanger [in'deindʒə]
to endorse [in'dɔːs]
to endorse a bill of exchange
He endorsed the plan/her opinion.
endorsee [ˌendɔː'siː]
endorsement [in'dɔːsmənt]
endorser [in'dɔːsə]
endowment [in'daumənt]
endowment funds
to enforce [in'fɔːs]
to enforce a law
to enforce a claim
enforced sale
enforcement [in'fɔːsmənt]
engaged [in'geidʒd]
He is engaged in business.
engaged signal
The number is engaged.
My time is fully engaged.
engagement [in'geidʒmənt]
I have another engagement.
engagement book
engineer [ˌendʒi'niə]
consulting engineer
engineering [ˌendʒi'niəriŋ]
engineering facilities pl
to enlarge (upon) [in'laːdʒ]
I don't want to enlarge upon the matter.
He enlarged his business.
enlargement [in'laːdʒmənt]
to enrol(l) [in'roul]
to enrol workers
to ensure [in'ʃuə]
to entail [in'teil]
That entails great expense.
enterprise ['entəpraiz]
business enterprise
free enterprise
a man of enterprise
enterprising ['entəpraiziŋ]
entitled [in'taitld]
He is entitled to vote.
entrepreneur [ˌɔntrəprə'nəː]
to entrust (with) [in'trʌst]
He was entrusted with the sale.
entry ['entri]
He made an entry in the book.
double-entry book-keeping
credit/debit entry
upon entry
no entry
entry form
entry visa
envelope ['enviloup]
to put a letter into an envelope
window envelope
equally ['iːkwəli]
to equip [i'kwip]
equipment [i'kwipmənt]

factory equipment
office equipment
equities *pl* ['ekwitiz]
equivalent [i'kwivələnt]
  What is $10 equivalent to in German
  money?
error ['erə]
  in error
  Errors excepted.
essentials *pl* [i'senʃəlz]
to establish [is'tæbliʃ]
  The business was established in 1910.
  He has established himself as a lawyer.
establishment [is'tæbliʃmənt]
  banking establishment
  industrial establishment
estate [is'teit]
  real estate
  estate agent
estimate ['estimit]
  a rough estimate
  to make an estimate of the costs
to estimate ['estimeit]
estimation [,esti'meiʃən]
  in my estimation
to evade [i'veid]
  He evaded the question.
to evaluate [i'væljueit]
evaluation [i,vælju'eiʃən]
evidence ['evidəns]
  for lack of evidence
  to give evidence
evident ['evidənt]
  It was evident to all of them that . . . .
ex [eks]
  ex factory/quay/warehouse/works
  ex interest
to exaggerate [ig'zædʒəreit]
to exceed [ik'si:d]
  He exceeded the speed limit.
except [ik'sept]
exception [ik'sepʃən]
  with the exception of
  an exception to the rule
  The exception proves the rule.
exceptional [ik'sepʃənl]
  exceptional offer
excess [ik'ses]
  to excess
  excess luggage Br/*baggage* Am
excessive [ik'sesiv]
  an excessive amount
exchange [iks'tʃeindʒ]
  bill of exchange
  foreign exchange
  exchange rate
  (telephone) exchange
to exclude from [iks'klu:d]
exclusive [iks'klu:siv]
  exclusive agent

to have exclusive use of s. th.
to have the exclusive rights
executive [ig'zekjutiv]
  top executive
to exhibit [ig'zibit]
  to exhibit goods
exhibition [,eksi'biʃən]
  industrial exhibition
  exhibition hall
  exhibition stand
exhibitor [ig'zibitə]
exit ['eksit]
  exit permit
to expand [iks'pænd]
  He expanded his business.
expansion [iks'pænʃən]
  expansion of credit/of production
expenditure [iks'penditʃə]
  Limit your expenditure.
expense [iks'pens]
  at great expense
  at the company's expense
  after deduction of expenses
expert ['ekspə:t]
  expert opinion
to expire [iks'paiə]
  When does your passport expire?
export ['ekspɔ:t]
  chief exports pl
  export industry
  export permit
  export trade
to export [eks'pɔ:t]
exporter [eks'pɔ:tə]
express [iks'pres]
  express delivery
  to send a parcel express
to extend [iks'tend]
  to extend credit
  I should like to have my residence permit
  extended.
extension [iks'tenʃən]
  to request an extension
  extension of credit
  Extension 226, please.
extensive [iks'tensiv]
  He gave an extensive report.
external [eks'tə:nl]
  external trade
extra ['ekstrə]
  Packing and postage extra.
  Do you get extra pay for this job?
  to be charged extra
  extra charges pl
  extra work
extract [iks'trækt]

face value [,feis 'vælju:]
to facilitate [fə'siliteit]

120

to facilitate customs clearance
facilities *pl* [fə'silitiz]
  transport facilities
factor ['fæktə]
  foreign/home factor
  key factors pl
  safety factor
fact-finding ['fækt͵faindiŋ]
  fact-finding commission
factoring ['fæktəriŋ]
failure ['feiljə]
  failure to pay
fall [fɔ:l]
  a sudden fall in prices
familiar [fə'miljə]
  He is not familiar with it.
family ['fæmili]
  family allowance
  family name
fancy goods *pl* ['fænsi͵gudz]
fare [fɛə]
  What's the fare?
  full fare
  economy fare
faulty ['fɔ:lti]
favour, *Am* **favor** ['feivə]
feature ['fi:tʃə]
  distinctive feature
fee [fi:]
  entrance fee
figure ['figə]
  sales figure
file [fail]
  on file
  file number
  to file an application'
  filing cabinet
  filing clerk
final ['fainl]
  final date
  final item
  final result
finance [fai'næns]
  finance department
financial [fai'nænʃəl]
  financial adviser
  financial condition
  financial difficulties pl
  financial expert
  financial standing
  financial status/situation
  financial year
financing [fai'nænsiŋ]
findings *pl* ['faindiŋz]
fine [fain]
finished ['finiʃt]
  finished goods pl
  half-finished products pl
finishing ['finiʃiŋ]
  finishing industry

finishing process
first-class ['fə:st'klɑ:s]
  first-class references pl
  He travelled first-class.
first-hand ['fə:st'hænd]
  first-hand information
  to buy first-hand
first-rate ['fə:st'reit]
  first-rate quality
fiscal ['fiskəl]
  fiscal year
fitness ['fitnis]
  fitness test
fitter ['fitə]
fitting ['fitiŋ]
fixed [fikst]
  fixed assets pl
  fixed rate of interest
  fixed salary
fixtures *pl* ['fikstʃəz]
flexible ['fleksəbl]
  flexible policy
flight [flait]
  connecting flight
  flight ticket
floating ['floutiŋ]
  floating capital
flourishing ['flʌriʃiŋ]
  flourishing industry
  flourishing trade
to fluctuate ['flʌktjueit]
  Prices are fluctuating.
fluctuation ['flʌktju'eiʃən]
  fluctuations in demand/in the exchange
  rate/in prices
f.o.b. (free on board)
folder ['fouldə]
follow-up ['folou'ʌp]
  follow-up advertising
  follow-up letter
foodstuffs pl ['fu:dstʌfs]
fool-proof ['fu:l-pru:f]
forced [fɔ:st]
  forced landing
  forced sale
forecast ['fɔ:kɑ:st]
  weather forecast
foreign ['forin]
  foreign assets pl
  foreign department
  foreign currency
  foreign trade
forgery ['fɔ:dʒəri]
  forgery of documents
form [fɔ:m]
  application form
  booking form
  order form
fortnight ['fɔ:tnait]
  in a fortnight

fortnightly
forward ['fɔːwəd]
  Please forward.
  forward transaction
  forward rate
forwarding ['fɔːwədiŋ]
  forwarding agent
  forwarding charges pl
  forwarding department
  forwarding instructions pl
framework ['freimwəːk]
  within the framework of
fraudulent ['frɔːdjulənt]
  fraudulent bankruptcy
freight [freit]
  freight charges
  air freight
  sea freight
  freight rate
  freight train
  freight transportation
freeze [friːz]
  wage/price freeze
fringe benefits *pl* [frindʒ 'benefits]
frozen ['frouzn]
  frozen assets pl
  frozen food
to fulfil(l) [ful'fil]
  to fulfil a contract
  to fulfil a promise
full-time ['ful'taim]
  full-time job
function ['fʌŋkʃən]
  He has an important function within the
  firm.
  The machine is not functioning properly.
  administrative function
fund [fʌnd]
  No funds.
  for lack of funds
  pension fund
  sufficient funds pl
furthermore [fəːðə'mɔː]

gains *pl* [geinz]
  to make gains
gainful ['geinful]
  gainful employment
  He is gainfully employed.
gap [gæp]
  to fill/stop-gap
  dollar gap
gas [gæs]
  gas main
  gas station Am
gate [geit]
gauge [geidʒ]
general ['dʒenərəl]
  general delivery

general manager
general meeting
General Post Office
consul general
Consulate General
given ['givn]
  at a given time
  under the given conditions
  given name
goal [goul]
  investment goal
going ['gouiŋ]
  Going! going! gone!
goods *pl* [gudz]
  consumer goods pl
  goods pl *in process*
goodwill [gud'wil]
go-slow ['gou'slou]
grade [greid]
  high-grade
  low-grade
  grade label(l)ing
grant [grɑːnt]
  to grant a loan
  to grant permission
  grant-in-aid
gross [grous]
  gross amount
  gross earnings pl
  gross national product
  gross weight
group [gruːp]
  age group
  group discussion
  group insurance
growth [grouθ]
  rate of growth
  growth in consumption
guarantee [,gærən'tiː]
  to guarantee a bill
guarantor [,gærən'tɔː]
guidance ['gaidəns]
  for your guidance
  vocational guidance

handbill ['hændbil]
to handle ['hændl]
  to handle the correspondence
  to handle goods
harbour dues *pl* ['hɑːbə djuːz]
  harbour master/commissioner
hard cash [hɑːd kæʃ]
harden ['hɑːdən]
hardware ['hɑːd-wɛə]
haulage ['hɔːlidʒ]
  haulage contractor
hazard ['hæzəd]
heading ['hediŋ]
headline ['hedlain]

head office, headquarters
['hed'ɔfis, 'hed'kwɔ:təz]
heavy ['hevi]
heavy losses pl
heavy traffic
helicopter ['helikɔptə]
heliport ['helipɔ:t]
hesitate ['heziteit]
hidden defect ['hidn di'fekt]
highest bidder ['haiist 'bidə]
high-grade ['hai'greid]
hire ['haiə]
to hire a car
hire purchase
to buy on hire purchase
to hoard [hɔ:d]
holder ['houldə]
holder of a bill/of shares
holding company ['houdiŋ 'kʌmpəni]
home [houm]
home address
home demand
home market
home produce
honour, *Am* honor ['ɔnə]
In someone's honour.
hospitality [hɔspitæliti]
host [houst]
hotel reservation [hou'tel rezə'veiʃən]
hourly wages *pl* ['auəli 'weidʒiz]

idle ['aidl]
idle capacity
idle capital
illegal [i'li:gəl]
imitation [ˌimi'teiʃən]
immovable [i'mu:vəbl]
immovables pl
implement ['implimənt]
to imply [im'plai]
This implies . . . .
import ['impɔ:t]
import duty
import regulations
import trade
to import [im'pɔ:t]
importing country
importer [im'pɔ:tə]
inability [inə'biliti]
inactive [in'æktiv]
incentive [in'sentiv]
incentive bonus
incidentals *pl* [ˌinsi'dentlz]
included, including [in'kludid, in'kludiŋ]
postage included
including value-added tax
income ['inkʌm]
average income
earned income

unearned income
yearly income
income group
income tax
incorporated (Inc.) *Am* [in'kɔ:pəreitid]
increase ['inkri:s]
increase in the bank rate
increase in capital/in salary
price/wage increase
increasing [in'kri:siŋ]
increasing costs pl
increasingly
increment ['inkrimənt]
to incur [in'kə:]
to incur debts
to incur liabilities
to incur losses
indebted [in'detid]
He is indebted to me.
index ['indeks]
index card
index number
cost-of-living index
to indicate ['indikeit]
He indicated the direction.
as indicated
indirect [ˌindi'rekt]
indirect tax
indispensable for/to [ˌindis'pensəbl]
individual [ˌindi'vidjuəl]
individual case/member
induction [in'dʌkʃən]
industrial [in'dʌstriəl]
industrial accident
industrial potential
industrial wages pl
industrialize [in'dʌstriəlaiz]
inefficient [ˌini'fiʃənt]
inferior [in'fiəriə]
inferior goods pl
in an inferior position
inflation [in'fleiʃən]
inflationary [in'fleiʃnəri]
inflationary trend
initial [i'niʃəl]
initial capital/salary
initiative [i'niʃiətiv]
He took the initiative.
inland ['inlənd]
inquiry [in'kwaiəri]
to insert [in'sə:t]
to insert a coin in the slot
to insert in brackets
insolvent [in'sɔlvənt]
inspection [in'spekʃən]
for inspection
inspection test
to install [in'stɔ:l]
to install a telephone
installation [instə'leiʃən]

instalment [in'stɔ:lmənt]
  by instalments
  in monthly instalments
  first instalment
instance ['instəns]
  for instance
  in the first instance
institution [,insti'tju:ʃən]
  banking institution
to instruct [in'strʌkt]
instruction(s *pl*) [in'strʌkʃən(z)]
  according to instructions
insurance [in'ʃuərəns]
  to take out an insurance
  insurance agent
  insurance benefit
  insurance claim
  insurance company
  insurance policy
  insurance premium
  fire/life insurance
interest (in) ['intrist]
  to bear/to yield interest
  compound interest
  credit interest
  interest on capital/on deposit
  interest-bearing
to interfere [,intə'fiə]
  interfere with something
internal [in'tə:nl]
  internal trade
international [,intə(:)'næʃənl]
  international trade
  international reply coupon
interpreter [in'tə:pritə]
interview ['intəvju:]
introduction [,intrə'dʌkʃən]
  letter of introduction
introductory [,intrə'dʌktəri]
  introductory offer
  introductory price
  introductory remarks pl
inventory ['invəntri]
  to draw up an inventory
to invest [in'vest]
  to invest money
  invested capital
to investigate (into) [in'vestigeit]
investigation [in,vesti'geiʃən]
investment [in'vestmənt]
  long-term/short-term investment
  investment securities pl
  investment trust
investor [in'vestə]
invisible [in'vizəbl]
  invisible exports pl
invoice ['invɔis]
  commercial invoice
  consular invoice
  as per invoice

pro forma invoice
to involve (in) [in'vɔlv]
  He is involved in a lawsuit.
  for all parties involved
irregular [i'regjulə]
  at irregular intervals
irrevocable [i'revəkəbl]
issue ['iʃu:]
  bank of issue
  a point at issue
  to issue a bill of exchange
item ['aitem]
  a fast-selling/hard-to-sell item
  items pl on the agenda
itinerary [ai'tinərəri]

jet [dʒet]
job [dʒɔb]
  full-time job
  job description
joint [dʒɔint]
  joint action
  joint owner
journal ['dʒə:nl]
junior ['dʒu:njə]
  junior clerk
  junior partner
justification [,dʒʌstifi'keiʃən]

to keep [ki:p]
  to keep books/an account of expenses
  to keep a shop
key [ki:]
  key factor
  key industry/position
kind [kaind]
  of the same kind
  to pay in kind
know-how ['nouhau]
  industrial know-how

label ['leibl]
  He put labels on his luggage.
labour, *Am* labor ['leibə]
  shortage of labour
  unskilled/skilled labour
  cost of labour
  labour conditions pl
  labour exchange
  labour market
  labour relations pl
  labour-saving
labo(u)rer ['leibərə]
to land [lænd]
landing ['lændiŋ]
  landing-field
  landing-stage

to launch [lɔ:ntʃ]
  to launch a business
  to launch a product
  to launch into a discussion
lawsuit ['lɔ:sju:t]
lawyer ['lɔ:jə]
layout ['leiaut]
leader ['li:də]
leading ['li:diŋ]
  leading firm
leaflet ['li:flit]
learner ['lə:nə]
lease [li:s]
leaseholder ['li:shouldə]
ledger ['ledʒə]
  to enter in the ledger
legal ['li:gəl]
  He took legal action.
  legal adviser
  legal capacity
  legal department
  legal entity
legally ['li:gəli]
  legally binding
letter ['letə]
  by letter
  He answered/acknowledged receipt of
    her letter.
  to post a letter
  business letter
  capital letter
  express letter
  registered letter
  sales letter
  letter of application
  letter of credit
  letter of introduction
  letter-box
  letter-head
level ['levl]
  on the same level
  salary/price level
liability [,laiə'biliti]
  assets and liabilities pl
  limited liability
  liability insurance
liable for ['laiəbl]
  You are liable to meet with an accident.
  liable to taxation
licence, Am license ['laisəns]
  The firm applied for a licence.
  He was granted a licence.
  driving/driver's licence
  export/import licence
  licence plate
to license ['laisəns]
licensee [,laisən'si:]
lieu [lju:]
  in lieu of
life, pl lives [laif, -vz]

for life
life assurance/insurance
limit ['limit]
  lower/upper limit
  time limit
limitation [,limi'teiʃən]
limited (Ltd.) ['limitid]
  limited company
line [lain]
  What line is he in?
  They had to stand in line.
  Hold the line, please.
  line of business
liquid ['likwid]
  liquid assets pl
to liquidate ['likwideit]
liquidity [li'kwiditi]
load [loud]
  pay load
loan [loun]
to locate [lou'keit]
location [lou'keiʃən]
  They had to decide on the location of
    their new office.
to lodge [lɔdʒ]
  He lodged an appeal/a complaint/an
    objection.
  to lodge a credit
long [lɔŋ]
  long-distance call
  long-distance lorry driver
  long-term bond
  long-term contract
  long-range planning
look [luk]
  look forward to
loose [lu:s]
  loose-leaf book
lot [lɔt]
low [lou]
  He is low on funds.
  low-budget
  low-grade
  lowest price
to lower ['louə]
  to lower the rate of interest
luggage Br ['lʌgidʒ]
  We registered our luggage.
  luggage insurance
  luggage label
  luggage ticket
  luggage van
lump [lʌmp]
  lump sum

mail [meil]
  by mail
  by return mail
  Please mail the letters. Am
  The mail is delivered at 10 o'clock.

incoming/outgoing mail
mail-order house
mailing list
main [mein]
  main office
  main road
  mainly
to maintain [mein'tein]
  He maintained his claim/opinion.
  to maintain the roads
maintenance ['meintənəns]
  maintenance costs pl
  resale price maintenance
major ['meidʒə]
  the major part of his income
  major road
majority [mə'dʒɔriti]
  in the majority of cases
  They are in the majority.
  majority (of votes)
make [meik]
  What make is your car?
  It's a popular make.
  standard make
maker ['meikə]
to manage ['mænidʒ]
  He managed the business.
  managing director
management ['mænidʒmənt]
  industrial management
  senior management
  top management
  management consultant
manager ['mænidʒə]
  assistant manager
  personnel/staff manager
  sales manager
managerial [,mænə'dʒiəriəl]
  He has a managerial position.
manpower ['mænpauə]
  shortage of manpower
manufacture [,mænju'fæktʃə]
  large-scale manufacture
  manufactured goods pl
manufacturer [,mænju'fæktʃərə]
manufacturing [,mænju'fæktʃəriŋ]
  manufacturing industry
  manufacturing process
margin ['mɑːdʒin]
  indicated in the margin
  He allowed a margin for expenses.
  profit margin
maritime ['mæritaim]
  maritime trade/insurance
market ['mɑːkit]
  He is in the market for furniture.
  This item is now on the market.
  His house will come on the market.
  This item has a market.
  market price/value

market report
market research
marketing ['mɑːkitiŋ]
  marketing consultant
mass [mæs]
  mass media
  mass production
maturity [mə'tjuəriti]
  payable at/on maturity
maximum ['mæksiməm]
  maximum speed
  maximum wage
means pl [miːnz]
measure ['meʒə]
  to take legal measures
  measure of capacity
mechanical [mi'kænikəl]
medium, pl media ['miːdjəm, 'miːdjə]
  advertising media
  medium-priced goods pl
  medium-sized
meeting ['miːtiŋ]
membership ['membəʃip]
  membership card/list
memo(randum) ['meməu
(,memə'rændəm)]
  memo pad
merchandise ['məːtʃəndaiz]
merchant ['məːtʃənt]
  merchant bank/ship
to merge [məːdʒ]
merger ['məːdʒə]
message ['mesidʒ]
  sales message
messenger ['mesindʒə]
  messenger boy
method ['meθəd]
mid-week ['mid'wiːk]
mileage ['mailidʒ]
  mileage allowance
mineral ['minərəl]
minimum, pl -ma ['miniməm, -mə]
  subsistence minimum
  minimum price/wage
minor ['mainə]
  minor changes pl
  minor repairs pl
  minor matter
minority [mai'nɔriti]
  They are in the minority.
  minority group
minus ['mainəs]
minutes pl ['minits]
  minutes of the meeting
misinterpret ['mis'in'təːprit]
misunderstanding ['misʌndə'stændiŋ]
mode [moud]
to modernize ['mɔdənaiz]
modification [,mɔdifi'keiʃən]
  He made some modifications.

to modify ['mɔdifai]
to modify the terms of the lease
monetary ['mʌnitəri]
monetary reform
money ['mʌni]
He is short of money.
money market
money order (M.O.)
monopoly [mə'nɔpəli]
to hold a monopoly on s.th.
monthly ['mʌnθli]
monthly instalment/production/report/
salary
mortgage ['mɔ:gidʒ]
motion ['mouʃən]
to propose a motion
The motion to adjourn was adopted/
carried.
motor ['moutə]
motor-boat
motor-car
motorway
to move [mu:v]
I move that we adjourn.
movement ['mu:vmənt]
downward movement
upward movement
multiple ['mʌltipl]
municipal [mju(:)'nisipəl]
mutual ['mju:tʃuəl]
mutual aid
mutual consent
mutual interest

nation ['neiʃən]
nation-wide
national ['næʃənl]
national economy
nationality [,næʃə'næliti]
to nationalize ['næʃnəlaiz]
needs [ni:dz]
meet the needs of
negligence ['neglidʒəns]
negligible ['neglidʒəbl]
negotiable [ni'gouʃiəbl]
not negotiable
to negotiate [ni'gouʃieit]
to negotiate a sale
negotiation [ni,gouʃi'eiʃən]
Negotiations were broken off.
net [net]
net income
net proceeds pl
net profit
network ['netwə:k]
network of roads/of railways/of canals
to nominate ['nɔmineit]
They nominated their candidates.
non-delivery [,nɔndi'livəri]

non-stop flight ['nɔn'stɔp 'flait]
normal ['nɔ:məl]
normally
note [nout]
as per note
advice note
bank-note
credit/debit note
delivery note
note-book
note-paper
notice ['noutis]
subject to a month's notice
at short notice
He gave them notice.
notice-board
to notify ['noutifai]

oath [ouθ]
on/under oath
He swore an oath/took an oath.
object ['ɔbdʒikt]
with the object of
objection [əb'dʒekʃən]
She didn't raise any objections.
He has no objection.
objective [əb'dʒektiv]
obligation [,ɔbli'geiʃən]
no obligation
He took on several obligations.
He cannot meet his obligations.
to oblige [ə'blaidʒ]
Much obliged.
Could you oblige me with some informa-
tion?
to obtain [əb'tein]
occasional [ə'keiʒənl]
occupation [,ɔkju'peiʃən]
occupational [,ɔkju(:)'peiʃənl]
occupational category
occupational disease
offer ['ɔfə]
firm offer
favourable offer
He declined the offer.
to offer for sale
all-inclusive offer
office ['ɔfis]
branch/head office
office building/equipment
office hours pl
to omit [ou'mit]
open ['oupən]
The firm opened up new markets.
to open an account/a business
open-air stand
open competition
to operate ['ɔpəreit]
to operate on schedule

operating ['ɔpəreitiŋ]
  operating costs pl/*expenses* pl
  operating instructions pl
operation [,ɔpə'reiʃən]
  to put into/out of operation
  commercial operation
  continuous operation
operator ['ɔpəreitə]
opinion [ə'pinjən]
  expert opinion
  opinion poll
opportunity [ɔpə'tju:niti]
  I take this opportunity to welcome
  you.
optimistic [,ɔpti'mistik]
optimum ['ɔptiməm]
  optimum conditions pl
option ['ɔpʃən]
  He had no option.
order ['ɔ:də]
  firm order
  initial order
  by order
  made out to order
  trial order
  repeat order
  process an order
  He placed an order with the firm.
  They confirmed/filled the order.
  order book/form
  money/postal order
organization [,ɔ:gənai'zeiʃən]
to organize ['ɔ:gənaiz]
origin ['ɔridʒin]
  certificate of origin
outlet ['autlet]
outline ['autlain]
output ['autput]
  annual/daily output
outstanding [aut'stændiŋ]
  outstanding accounts pl
overall ['ouvərɔ:l]
  overall result
overdraft ['ouvədra:ft]
to overdraw o.'s account [,ouvə'drɔ:]
overdue ['ouvə'dju:]
  The aircraft is several hours overdue.
overhead ['ouvəhed]
  overheads pl, *overhead costs* pl/*expenses*
    pl
overseas ['ouvə'si:z]
  overseas market
oversight ['ouvəsait]
overtime ['ouvətaim]
  He worked overtime.

pack [pæk]
  a pack of cards
  factory-packed

package ['pækidʒ]
  package advertising
  package tour
packet ['pækit]
  Send me a packet of tea, please.
  registered packet
  wage packet
packing ['pækiŋ]
  not including packing
  packing paper
pad [pæd]
  writing pad
  ink pad
paid [peid]
  carriage paid
  duty-paid
pamphlet ['pæmflit]
paper ['peipə]
  to show one's papers
  He wrote a paper on the subject.
  paper-money
  paper-work
paragraph ['pærəgra:f]
parcel ['pa:sl]
  parcel delivery
  parcel office
  parcel post
parent company ['pɛərənt 'kʌmpəni]
part [pa:t]
  part payment
  part-time job
  part-time worker
participation [pa:tisipeiʃən]
particulars [pə'tikjuləz]
partner ['pa:tnə]
  senior/junior partner
  sleeping partner
partnership ['pa:tnəʃip]
party ['pa:ti]
  the parties concerned
  a third party
  party line
pass (to) [pa:s]
  The bill was passed.
  The firm passed from father to son.
  free pass
passage ['pæsidʒ]
  He booked a passage to New York.
passport ['pa:spɔ:t]
  passport control
patent (on) ['peitənt]
  patent leather shoes pl
  patent office
patron ['peitrən]
patronage ['pætrənidʒ]
pay [pei]
  to pay a bill
  to pay cash/by cheque
  to pay damages
  pay packet/roll

pay phone
pay rise
payable ['peiəbl]
payable at sight
payer ['peiə]
payment ['peimənt]
on payment
cash payment
payment in kind
terms pl of payment
peak [pi:k]
Their shares reached a new peak yesterday.
peak viewing hours pl
pension ['penʃən]
to pension off
old-age pension
pension fund
per [pə:]
as per
per annum
per capita
per post
per pro. (p.p.)
percentage [pə'sentidʒ]
performance [pə'fɔ:məns]
performance of a duty
period ['piəriəd]
for a period of two months
periodical [,piəri'ɔdikəl]
monthly/weekly periodical
perishable ['periʃəbl]
perishable goods pl
permanent ['pə:mənənt]
permission [pə'miʃən]
by special permission
permit ['pə:mit]
landing permit
personal ['pə:snl]
personal call
personal data
personal shares pl
personal status
personnel [,pə:sə'nel]
personnel department
personnel files pl
personnel manager
petty ['peti]
petty cash
phone [foun]
He contacted me by phone.
You are wanted on the phone.
photo-copy ['foutou,kɔpi]
piece-work ['pi:s-wə:k]
They do piece-work.
to pigeon-hole ['pidʒinhoul]
pipeline ['paip-lain]
place [pleis]
place of business
place of payment/of performance

to place an order
to place shares
planning ['plæniŋ]
plant [plɑ:nt]
plant manager
power plant
pledge [pledʒ]
He pledged his property.
plus [plʌs]
pocket ['pɔkit]
He is out of pocket.
He pocketed all the profits.
pocketbook
pocket book (edition)
pocket money
point [pɔint]
He pointed out a problem.
policy ['pɔlisi]
They adopted a new policy.
It is my policy to . . . .
marketing policy
pool [pu:l]
The partners pooled the profits.
Let's pool our savings/our resources.
the football pools pl
motor pool
population [,pɔpju'leiʃən]
population movement
a fall/rise in population
port [pɔ:t]
to call at a port
port of destination
port of registry
position [pə'ziʃən]
position as per December 31st
financial/legal position
positive ['pɔzitiv]
I'm positive that he will come.
post [poust]
They kept us posted.
postcode
post-free
postman
post office
post-office box, P.O.B.
postage ['poustidʒ]
postage paid
postal ['poustəl]
postal order
poste restante ['poust'restɑ:nt]
to postpone [poust'poun]
postscript, P.S. ['pousskript]
potential [pou'tenʃəl]
industrial potential
potential sales pl
power ['pauə]
power of attorney
power consumption
power station
power supply

buying/purchasing power
financial power
precaution [pri'kɔːʃən]
to predict [pri'dikt]
preferably ['prefərebli]
preference ['prefərəns]
What are your preferences?
preference share
preferential [,prefə'renʃəl]
preferential claim
preliminary [pri'liminəri]
preliminary discussion
preliminary remarks pl
premises pl ['premisiz]
on the premises
business premises
premium ['priːmjəm]
to put a premium on s.th.
to sell at a premium
insurance premium
prepaid ['priːpeid]
preparation [prepə'reiʃən]
in preparation for his visit
to present [pri'zent]
He presented the facts as they really
were.
to present a bill for acceptance
to present a cheque at the bank
presentation [,prezen'teiʃən]
payable on presentation
president ['prezidənt]
pressing ['presiŋ]
pressure ['preʃə]
They put/brought pressure to bear on
him.
economic pressure
pressure of taxation
pressure group
to presume [pri'zjuːm]
I presume he is at the office.
presumption [pri'zʌmpʃən]
previous ['priːvjəs]
The previous day was a holiday.
previous experience
previous month/year
price [prais]
at the current market price
at a reduced price
asked/bid price
price ceiling
price control
price cut
price freeze
price list
price maintenance
price stability
primarily ['praimərili]
primary ['praiməri]
That's of primary importance.
primary education

primary products pl
principal ['prinsipl]
principal creditor/debtor
principal and interest
principle ['prinsipl]
on principle
He stuck to his principles.
print [print]
in print
out of print
to appear in print
Please print your name.
printed matter
prior (to) ['praiə]
prior to any discussion
subject to prior sale
priority [prai'ɔriti]
We shall give high priority to your order.
He was given priority.
of top priority
priority list
to take priority over
private ['praivit]
procedure [prə'siːdʒə]
usual procedure
proceeds pl ['prousiːdz]
cash proceeds
process ['prouses]
in the process of construction
manufacturing process
processing ['prousesiŋ]
processing industry
produce ['prɔdjuːs]
to produce [prə'djuːs]
product ['prɔdʌkt]
intermediate product
national product
production [prə'dʌkʃən]
The plant goes into production tomorrow.
We had to curb production.
production costs pl
production manager
production planning
productivity [,prɔdʌk'tiviti]
to increase productivity
professional [prə'feʃənl]
professional man
professional qualifications pl
professional training
proficiency [prə'fiʃənsi]
profit ['prɔfit]
to make a profit
He sold the house at a profit.
clear profit
profit and loss account
profit margin
profit-sharing
profitable ['prɔfitəbl]
pro forma [prou'fɔːmə]
pro forma invoice

program(me) ['prougræm]
(computer) program(me)
manufacturing program(me)
programmer ['prougræmə]
progressive [prou'gresiv]
progressive tax
project ['prɔdʒekt]
to carry out a project
housing project
to project [prə'dʒekt]
promissory ['prɔmisəri]
promissory note
to promote [prə'mout]
to promote a company
to promote a product
promotion [prə'mouʃən]
export/sales promotion
promotion manager
prompt [prɔmpt]
a prompt answer/reply
prompt delivery
property ['prɔpəti]
industrial property
personal property
landed property
proportion [prə'pɔ:ʃən]
in proportion to
to be out of proportion to
proposal [prə'pouzəl]
to make/to reject a proposal
to propose [prə'pouz]
to propose an amendment
proprietor [prə'praiətə]
sole proprietor
prospect ['prɔspekt]
He has no prospect of success.
prospective [prəs'pektiv]
prospective buyer/client
prospectus [prəs'pektəs]
prosperity [prɔs'periti]
prosperous ['prɔspərəs]
protective [prə'tektiv]
protective duty
protective measures pl
to provide (for) [prə'vaid]
to provide cover
provided that . . . .
provision [prə'viʒən]
with the usual provisions
He made provision for his old age.
final provisions pl
provisional [prə'viʒənl]
They made a provisional arrangement.
public ['pʌblik]
in public
public opinion
public relations pl
public utility
publication [pʌbli'keiʃən]
publicity [pʌb'lisiti]

publicity department/manager
to publish ['pʌbliʃ]
publisher ['pʌbliʃə]
to punch [pʌntʃ]
punch card
purchase ['pə:tʃəs]
purchase price
purchase tax
purchasing power
put [put]
to put off
to put up with

qualification (for) [,kwɔlifi'keiʃən]
without any qualification
He has the necessary qualifications.
professional qualifications pl
qualified ['kwɔlifaid]
He is not qualified for this position.
quality ['kwɔliti]
to guarantee the quality of a product
inferior/superior quality
quality control/goods pl
quantity ['kwɔntiti]
quarter ['kwɔ:tə]
business/residential quarter
quarterly
query ['kwiəri]
questionnaire [,kwestʃə'nɛə]
He filled in the questionnaire.
quota ['kwoutə]
quotation [kwou'teiʃən]
to quote [kwout]
Please quote ref. (reference).
to be quoted officially

railway, *Am* **railroad** ['reilwei, 'reilroud]
railway carriage
railway crossing
railway guide
railway junctions
railway station
random ['rændəm]
at random
random sample
range [reindʒ]
The shop keeps a wide range of goods.
price range
rapid ['ræpid]
rapid growth/decline
rate [reit]
flat rate
at a cheap rate
at the most favourable rate
at the present rate
at a reduced rate
rate of discount
rate of exchange

rate of interest
bank rate
birth/death rate
ratio ['reiʃiou]
in the ratio of 2: 1
cover ratio
rationalization [,ræʃnəlai'zeiʃən]
to rationalize ['ræʃnəlaiz]
raw [rɔ:]
raw material
re [ri:]
ready ['redi]
to find a ready market
ready-made clothes pl
ready money
real [riəl]
real estate
real silk
real wage(s)
to realize ['riəlaiz]
rebate ['ri:beit]
receipt [ri'si:t]
against receipt
on receipt of the draft
He acknowledged receipt of the letter.
receiver [ri'si:və]
receiver (of stolen goods)
reception [ri'sepʃən]
He held a reception for the visitors
reception desk
receptionist [ri'sepʃənist]
recession [ri'seʃən]
receipt [ri'siit]
recipient [ri'sipient]
to reckon ['rekən]
to reckon with s. th.
to reckon upon s. th.
I reckon that . . . .
recommendation [,rekəmen'deiʃən]
letter of recommendation
record ['rekɔ:d]
off the record
He kept a careful record of all
expenses.
recording [ri'kɔ:diŋ]
recruitment [ri'kruitmənt]
rectify ['rektifai]
to reduce [ri'dju:s]
at a reduced price/rate
We must reduce costs/expenses.
He reduced his stocks.
reduction [ri'dʌkʃən]
reduction of expenses
to refer (to) [ri'fə:]
referring to your letter
reference ['refrəns]
with reference to
He has excellent references.
You may quote me as a reference.
your/our reference

reference book
reference number
refund ['ri:fʌnd]
to refund [ri:'fʌnd]
The shopkeeper refunded the full price.
refusal [ri'fju:zəl]
a flat refusal
regard [ri'ga:d]
with regard to your letter of
regarding [ri'ga:diŋ]
regardless of [ri'ga:dlis]
regardless of expense
region ['ri:dʒən]
regional ['ri:dʒənl]
register (at, with) ['redʒistə]
He registered at the hotel.
registered trade-mark
cash register
commercial register
a registered letter
Registered!
registration [,redʒis'treiʃən]
registration of luggage
registration desk
registration fee/form
regulation [,regju'leiʃən]
according to/contrary to regulations
traffic regulations pl
to reject [ri'dʒekt]
The motion was rejected.
to reject a cheque/an offer
rejection [ri'dʒekʃən]
relating to [ri'leitiŋ]
relations pl [ri'leiʃənz]
to break off all relations
business relations pl
relative ['relətiv]
reliability [ri,laiə'biliti]
reliable [ri'laiəbl]
It's a reliable firm.
relocate [,ri:lou'keit]
to rely on [ri'lai]
You can rely on him.
remainder [ri'meində]
remedy ['remidi]
reminder [ri'maində]
letter of reminder
to remit [ri'mit]
He remitted the £2 through his bank.
to remit by cheque
remittance [ri'mitəns]
to make a remittance
remittance order
removal (to) [ri'mu:vəl]
removal (of business)
removal van
remuneration [ri'mju:nə'reiʃən]
to renew [ri'nju:]
He renewed the bill/the contract.
He should renew his efforts.

renewal [ri'nju(:)əl]
renewal bill

rent [rent]
We pay £30 rent a month.
rent-a-car

rental ['rentl]

reorganization ['ri:,ɔ:gənai'zeiʃən]

to reorganize ['ri:'ɔ:gənaiz]

to repay ['ri:'pei]

repayment [ri:'peimənt]

replacable [ri'pleisəbl]

replacement [ri'pleismənt]
replacement cost/price
replacement parts pl

report (on) [ri'pɔ:t]
He gave a detailed report.
market report

to represent [,repri'zent]
Mr. Fox will represent the firm.
to be represented on the board

representation [,reprizen'teiʃən]

representative [,repri'zentətiv]
authorized representative

reputation [,repju(:)'teiʃən]

request [ri'kwest]
by/on request
He came at my request.
request for payment

to require [ri'kwaiə]
They require extra help.

requirements (of) pl [ri'kwaiəmənts]
It meets our requirements.

resale ['ri:'seil]
resale price

research [ri'sə:tʃ]
He does research work.

reservation [,rezə'veiʃən]
without reservation
We could not get hotel reservations.

reserve [ri'zə:v]
all rights reserved
hidden reserves pl

to resign [ri'zain]
He has resigned as chairman.

resignation [,rezig'neiʃən]
He sent in his resignation.

resolution [,rezə'lu:ʃən]
The members adopted the resolution unanimously.

resources pl [ri'sɔ:siz]
He was left to his own resources.
natural resources pl

respectively [ris'pektivli]

responsibility [ris,pɔnsə'biliti]
to delegate responsibility to s.o.
He took the responsibility.

responsible [ris'pɔnsəbl]
He was held responsible for the damage.

to restock ['ri:'stɔk]

to restrict (to) [ris'trikt]
They restricted membership.

result [ri'zʌlt]

restriction [ris'trikʃən]
without restrictions
import restriction/restriction on imports

retail (trade) ['ri:teil treid]
to sell wholesale and retail
retail dealer/price

retailer [ri:'teilə]

to retire [ri'taiə]
He has retired (from work).

return [ri'tə:n]
return air fare
by return of post
in return for
income tax return
return postage

revaluation ['ri:vælju'eiʃən]

revenue office ['revinju: 'ɔfis]

reverse [ri'və:s]
on the reverse
He reversed the car.
reverse side

review [ri'vju:]
month under review

rise [raiz]
rise in prices/in wages

risk [risk]
at one's own risk
He took no risks.
risk of loss

rival ['raivəl]
rival business/firm

rough [rʌf]
rough calculation
rough estimate

routine [ru:'ti:n]
routine work

run (on) [rʌn]
in the long run
trial run
The licence has two months to run.
to run a factory

running ['rʌniŋ]
running costs pl
running expenses pl

rush [rʌʃ]
rush hour

sack [sæk]
to get the sack

safe [seif]
That's a safe estimate.
to be on the safe side
safe-deposit box

safety ['seifti]
They were brought to safety.
road safety

safety factor
safety measures pl
salary ['sæləri]
He holds a salaried position.
He is a salaried man/an employee.
increase in salary
top salary
salary bracket
sale [seil]
sales conscious
not for sale
salesgirl/salesman
sales manager
sales promotion
salesroom
sales talk
saleable, Am **salable** ['seiləbl]
salutation [sælju'teiʃən]
sample ['saːmpl]
by sample post
up to sample
free sample
sample book
satisfactory [ˌsætis'fæktəri]
to save [seiv]
saving ['seiviŋ]
He withdrew his savings from the bank.
savings account/bank
savings deposit
scale [skeil]
to scale
on a large scale
drawn to a scale of 1 : 10
wage scale
scarce [skɛəs]
Eggs are scarce at the moment.
schedule ['ʃedjuːl, Am 'skedjuːl]
on/behind schedule
We are scheduled to leave at 8 o'clock.
scheme [skiːm]
company pension scheme
He has a scheme for raising the money.
scope [skoup]
seasonal ['siːzənl]
seasonal demand/unemployment
seaworthy [siː'wəːθi]
second ['sekənd]
to second the motion
secondary ['sekəndəri]
That's a matter of secondary importance.
secondary effect
secretarial [ˌsekrə'tɛəriəl]
secretarial work
section ['sekʃən]
residential section
section 4
sector ['sektə]
secure (on, by) [si'kjuə]
secured by mortgage
secure investments pl

security [si'kjuəriti]
against security
to provide security
to lend money on security
security market
select [si'lekt]
to select a team
selected goods pl
selection [si'lekʃən]
They have a large selection of shoes.
self, pl **selves** [self, selvz]
a cheque drawn to self
self-contained house
self-employed
self-service (store)
self-service restaurant
self-supporting
to sell (at) (sold, sold) [sel, sould]
The store is sold out.
He sold the house at a profit.
The shirts are selling well.
seller ['selə]
seller's market
selling ['seliŋ]
hard selling
selling methods pl
selling order/price
semi-finished ['semi'finiʃt]
semi-finished product
semi-skilled ['semi'skild]
semi-skilled worker
sender ['sendə]
senior (to) ['siːnjə]
senior clerk/partner
separate ['seprit]
separate account/print
by separate mail (Am)
to separate ['sepəreit]
series, pl **series** ['siəriːz]
in series
service (to) ['səːvis]
railway/shipping service
service station
service engineer
set [set]
at a set time
set of cutlery
to settle (with) ['setl]
All claims were settled.
to settle an account
settlement ['setlmənt]
in settlement of all claims
in settlement of your account
They came to/reached a settlement.
an out-of-court settlement
to set up ['set 'ʌp]
to set up in business
set-up ['setʌp]
share [ʃɛə]
to share equally

They shared the costs.
He holds shares in the company.
shareholder ['ʃɛə,houldə]
shift (to) [ʃift]
The men on the night shift work from
10 p.m. to 6 a.m.
ship [ʃip]
The goods were shipped to New York on
Friday.
shipment ['ʃipmənt]
ready for shipment
shipping ['ʃipiŋ]
shipping clerk
shipping department
shipping company
shipping documents pl
shipping instructions pl
shop [ʃɔp]
He opened/set up a shop.
shop assistant
shopkeeper
shop-window
shopping ['ʃɔpiŋ]
She has a lot of shopping to do.
shopping centre
shortage (of) ['ʃɔ:tidʒ]
food shortage
housing shortage
shortage of money
shortage of personnel
shortage of manpower
shorthand typist ['ʃɔ:thænd]
short-term ['ʃɔ:ttə:m]
short-term credit
short-term loan
short-time (work) ['ʃɔ:ttaim]
showroom ['ʃəurum]
sight [sait]
30 days after sight
payable at sight
bill payable at sight
signature ['signitʃə]
silent ['sailənt]
silent partner
site [sait]
site of an industry
site plan
situation [,sitju'eiʃən]
economic situation
situations vacant
situations wanted
skilled (at, in) [skild]
skilled labour
skilled workman
sleeping ['sli:piŋ]
sleeping accommodation
sleeping car, sleeper
sleeping partner
slip [slip]
paying-in slip

slip of the pen
slogan ['slougən]
slump [slʌmp]
slump in production
social ['souʃəl]
social background
social insurance/security
social legislation
social security benefit
social services pl
social welfare
society [sə'saiəti]
building society
co-operative society Br
soft [sɔft]
soft currency
soft drinks pl
sole [soul]
sole agency/agent
sole bill of exchange
solely responsible
solution [sə'lu:ʃən]
a workable solution
solvency ['sɔlvənsi]
solvent ['sɔlvənt]
source [sɔ:s]
from a reliable source
source of funds/income
source of supply
space [speis]
in the space of a year
advertising space
a blank space
space industry
spare [spɛə]
I don't have a minute to spare.
spare part
spare capacity
spare time
special ['speʃəl]
special delivery Am
special offer
special train
specialist ['speʃəlist]
to specialize in ['speʃəlaiz]
specific [spi'sifik]
on a specific day
a specific statement
specification [,spesifi'keiʃən]
to specify ['spesifai]
He specified the exact measurements.
specimen ['spesimin]
specimen copy/letter
to speculate (for/on) ['spekjuleit]
He speculated in shares/for a fall.
speculation [,spekju'leiʃən]
speculation in real estate/in stocks
to speed (sped, sped) [spi:d, sped]
He is always speeding.
to speed up production

speed limit
spending ['spendiŋ]
  spending money
  spending power
sphere [sfiə]
  sphere of activity
  sphere of interest
spiral ['spaiərel]
  wage-price spiral
sponsor ['sponsə]
spot [spot]
  spot business
  spot cash
  spot goods pl
squeeze [skwi:z]
  credit squeeze
stability [stə'biliti]
  monetary stability
  price stability
staff [stɑːf]
  He is on the staff of the firm.
  staff manager
  staff shortage
stage [steidʒ]
  at this stage
  in stages
stamp [stæmp]
  date/official stamp
  internal revenue stamp
  stamp duty
  stamp collection
  stamp collector
  stamp dealer
stand [stænd]
  newspaper stand
  cabstand
standard ['stændəd]
  above/below standard
  by present-day standards
  to be up to standard
  standard of living
  standard size
  standard time
standing ['stændiŋ]
  standing committee
  standing order
  standing room
standstill ['stændstil]
  Work in the factory has come to a standstill.
staple ['steipl]
  staple commodities pl
to state [steit]
  as stated above
  State full particulars.
  at the stated time
statement ['steitmənt]
  according to/as per statement
  He made a statement on oath that . . . .
  Do you wish to make a statement?

bank/cash statement
  statement of account
  statement of finances
stationery ['steiʃnəri]
statistical [stə'tistikəl]
  to record statistically
statistics pl [stə'tistiks]
  commercial/trade statistics
status ['steitəs]
  personal/marital status
  financial status
statutory ['stætjutəri]
  statutory holiday
stencil ['stensl]
step [step]
  step by step
  This is a great step forward.
  to take steps (to do s. th.)
  to step up production
to stipulate ['stipjuleit]
  as stipulated
stock [stok]
  We don't stock that brand.
  in (out of) stock
  to take stock
  His stock has gone up.
  live/dead stock
  rolling stock
  stockbroker
  stock exchange
  stockholder
  stock-in-trade
  stock list
  stock market
  stock-taking
storage ['stɔːridʒ]
  in storage
  cold storage
  storage charges pl/*room*
store [stɔː]
  ex store
  in store
  chain store
  department store
to streamline ['striːmlain]
stress [stres]
strict [strikt]
  strictly confidential
  in the strictest sense of the word
  strictly speaking
strike [straik]
  The workers are going on strike/are on strike.
structure ['strʌktʃə]
  economic structure
  price structure
study group ['stʌdi 'gruːp]
style [stail]
  business style
  the latest style

subject ['sʌbdʒikt]
to change the subject
subject to approval/to your consent
Prices are subject to change without
  notice.
Subject:
to submit [səb'mit]
He submitted a plan/a report.
to submit a proposal
to subscribe (for/to) [səb'skraib]
to subscribe to a newspaper
subscriber [səb'skraibə]
subscriber's number
subscription [səb'skripʃən]
by subscription
to invite subscriptions for a loan
subsequently ['sʌbsikwəntli]
subsidiary [səb'sidjəri]
subsidiary agreement
to subsidize ['sʌbsidaiz]
substantial [səb'stænʃəl]
a substantial improvement
a substantial progress
substitute (for) ['sʌbstitju:t]
to subtract [səb'trækt]
to sue for [sju:, su:]
to sue for damages
suggestion [sə'dʒestʃən]
His suggestion is that . . . .
It's only a suggestion.
suit [sju:t]
to bring/institute a suit against s.o.
suitable [sju:təbl]
to suit (to) [sju:t]
He is suited to the job of salesman.
The date doesn't suit me.
sum [sʌm]
a sum of $50
lump sum
sum total
to sum up (to) ['sʌm 'ʌp]
Let me sum up briefly.
sundries pl ['sʌndri:z]
sundry ['sʌndri]
sundry expenses pl
superior (to) [sju(:)'piəriə]
Our new typewriter is superior to the old
  one.
of superior quality
Is he her superior?
to supervise ['sju:pəvaiz]
supervision (of) [,sju:pə'viʒən]
close supervision
supervisor ['sju:pəvaizə]
supplement (to) ['sʌplimənt]
supplementary [,sʌpli'mentəri]
supplementary agreement
supplementary order
supplier [sə'plai-ə]
main supplier

supply (to) [sə'plai]
They supply us with shirts.
The supply of stockings cannot meet the
  demand.
We are running out of supplies.
office supplies pl
power supply
supply and demand
supply price
support [sə'po:t]
in support of my motion
to support a project
financial support
surcharge ['sə:tʃɑ:dʒ]
surplus ['sə:pləs]
budget surplus
export/import surplus
surplus population
surplus weight
survey (of) ['sə:vei]
He made a general survey of the situation/
  of the market.
to survey [sə:'vei]
switch (to) [switʃ]
to switch over production
switchboard
syndicate ['sindikit]
banking syndicate
synthetic [sin'θetik]
synthetic fibre
system ['sistim]
banking system
metric system
system of railways

tab [tæb]
to keep tabs on
table ['teibl]
to table a motion
table of contents
table of exchange rates/of charges
tacit ['tæsit]
tacit approval
tag [tæg]
price tag
taker ['teikə]
takings pl ['teikiŋz]
tally ['tæli]
tally sheet
tape [teip]
tape-recorder
punched tape
target ['tɑ:git]
sales target
tariff ['tærif]
as per tariff
tariff barriers pl
tariff protection
tariff regulations pl

tax (on) [tæks]
corporation tax
income tax
taxpayer
taxation [tæk'seiʃən]
subject to taxation
team [ti:m]
teamwork
technical ['teknikəl]
technical difficulties pl
technician [tek'niʃən]
technique [tek'ni:k]
technology [tek'nɔlədʒi]
telecommunications pl
['teli-kə,mju(:)ni'keiʃənz]
telegram ['teligræm]
by telegram
telephone ['telifoun]
on the telephone
He does all his business by telephone.
telephone call
telephone conversation
telephone directory
telephonist [ti'ləfonist]
teleprinter, *Am* teletypewriter
['teli,printə, teli'taip,raitə]
by teleprinter
television ['teli,viʒən]
television advertising
television audience
television broadcast
television station
telex ['teleks]
teller ['telə]
temporary ['tempərəri]
temporary credit
tenant ['tenənt]
landlord and tenant
to tend (to, towards) [tend]
tendency ['tendənsi]
downward/upward tendency
tender ['tendə]
by tender
*The company invited tenders for the
project.*
to tender one's resignation
legal tender
tentatively ['tentətivli]
term [tə:m]
under the terms of the article
term of office
on easy terms
He only thinks in terms of money.
What are your terms?
terms of delivery/of payment
long-/short-term
subscription terms pl
terminal ['tə:minl]
air terminal
bus terminal

testify ['testifai]
testimonial ['testi'mounjəl]
textiles pl ['tekstailz]
theft [θeft]
to be guilty of theft
theft insurance
theft risk
ticket ['tikit]
to buy a ticket
price ticket
boarding/landing ticket
ticket office
tight [tait]
tight money market
Money is tight.
time [taim]
at a given time
overtime
Your time is up.
time of arrival
time bargain
time limit
timetable
timing ['taimiŋ]
title to ['taitl]
title deed
ton [tʌn]
by the ton
top [tɔp]
top executive
top-grade quality
top management
top salary
topic ['tɔpik]
total ['toutl]
to total up expenses
sum total
total receipts pl/*value*
total weight
tour [tuə]
conducted/package tour
tour of inspection
tourism ['tuərizm]
tourist ['tuərist]
tourist agency/office
tourist class
tourist industry
trade [treid]
He is a carpenter by trade.
*This article is only supplied to the
trade.*
He does a good trade.
He traded in his used car.
foreign/home trade
trade and industry
trade-mark
trade name
trade union
trader ['treidə]
trading ['treidiŋ]

trading company
trading stamp
traffic (in) ['træfik]
air traffic
freight traffic
heavy traffic
traffic control/jam
traffic light
traffic regulations pl
trained [treind]
trained personnel
trainee [trei'ni:]
training ['treiniŋ]
training period
transaction [træn'zækʃən]
cash transaction
transfer ['trænsfə(:)]
transfer deed
to transfer [træns'fə:]
He transferred the money to his brother's
    account.
to transfer by endorsement
to transform [træns'fɔ:m]
transit ['trænsit]
dammaged/lost in transit
transit of goods
transit camp
transit duty
transit traffic/visa
translator [træns'leitə]
transmission [trænz'miʃən]
transmission of news
transmission of a radio/television
    programme
to transmit [trænz'mit]
to transmit a message
transport ['trænspɔ:t]
door-to-door transport
rail/road transport
cost of transport
to transport [træns'pɔt]
Our goods are transported by plane.
transportation [,trænspɔ:'teiʃən]
Do you have transportation? Am
    freight transportation
    transportation rate
travel (for) ['trævl]
He is travelling on business.
travel agent's/agency/bureau
traveller, Am **traveler** ['trævlə]
commercial traveller
traveller's cheque, Am traveler's check
travelling ['trævliŋ]
travelling salesman
travelling bag/case
travelling clock
travelling expenses pl
treasurer ['treʒərə]
treaty ['tri:ti]
commercial treaty

trend [trend]
downward/upward trend
trend of prices
trial ['traiəl]
on trial
Give him a month's trial.
trial period
trial order
triplicate ['triplikit]
in triplicate
truly ['tru:li]
I am truly sorry.
Yours (very) truly/Very truly yours
. . . . Am
trust (in) [trʌst]
in/on trust
to turn over [tə:n]
He turns over $10,000 a week.
turnover ['tə:n,ouvə]
last year's turnover
turnover tax
type [taip]
in bold type
typewriter
typist ['taipist]

unacceptable ['ʌnək'septəbl]
unanimous [ju(:)'næniməs]
His proposal was accepted with unanimous
    approval.
unauthorized ['ʌn'ɔ:θəraizd]
unconditional [,ʌnkən'diʃənl]
under ['ʌndə]
under no circumstances
under the provisions of the law
under separate cover
The road is under construction.
Is everything under control?
undergo ['ʌndə'gou]
to underrate [,ʌndə'reit]
understaffed [,ʌndə'sta:ft]
We are understaffed.
understanding [,ʌndə'stændiŋ]
on the understanding that . . . .
They came to an understanding with the
firm.
to undertake (-took, -taken) [,ʌndə'teik]
to undertake to do s.th.
undertaking [,ʌndə'teikiŋ]
industrial undertaking
unemployed ['ʌnim'plɔid]
unemployed capital
the unemployed
unemployment ['ʌnim'plɔimənt]
unemployment benefit/compensation/
relief
union ['ju:njən]
Universal Postal Union
trade union

139

union rights pl
unit ['ju:nit]
  unit of account
  unit furniture
  unit price
unlawful ['ʌn'lɔ:ful]
unlimited [ʌn'limitid]
  for an unlimited period
to unload ['ʌn'loud]
  to unload a ship
unofficial ['ʌnə'fiʃəl]
  unofficial news (mit sing)
unpaid ['ʌn'peid]
  unpaid capital
  unpaid interest
unprofitable [ʌn'prɔfitəbl]
unreliable ['ʌnri'laiəbl]
unskilled ['ʌn'skild]
  unskilled worker
up-to-date ['ʌptədeit]
  pred up to date ['–'-]
  Are your books up to date?
upkeep ['ʌpki:p]
upward(s *adv*) ['ʌpwəd(-z)]
  Prices are tending upwards.
  upward movement/trend
urban ['ə:bən]
  urban area
urgent ['ə:dʒənt]
usage ['ju:zidʒ]
  commercial usage
use [ju:s]
  in common use
  ready for use
  Is this of any use to you?
  to come into use
  to go out of use
  instructions pl for use
useful ['ju:sful]
user ['ju:zə]
  ultimate user
utility [ju(:)'tiliti]
  marginal utility
  utility goods pl
to utilize ['ju:tilaiz]

vacancy ['veikənsi]
  to fill a vacancy
vacant ['veikənt]
  He applied for the vacant position.
  vacant possession
vacation [və'keiʃən]
  He is on vacation. Am
valid ['vælid]
  valid until recalled
  to become valid
  valid argument
  valid claim
value ['vælju:]

  for value received . . . .
  book/commercial value
  value-added tax
variable ['vɛəriəbl]
  variable cost
variety [və'raiəti]
  a wide variety of hats
to vary ['vɛəri]
  varying prices pl
venture ['vəntʃə]
  He has a share in the venture.
verbally ['və:bəli]
version ['və:ʃən]
vested interest/right
  ['vestid 'intrist/rait]
vice-chairman/-president
  ['vais'tʃɛəmən/'prezidənt]
view (of, on) [vju:]
  in my view
  Our views differ.
  viewpoint
visa ['vi:zə]
visible ['vizəbl]
  visible imports pl
visitor ['vizitə]
  visitor's book
vocational [vou'keiʃnl]
  vocational guidance
  vocational training
void [vɔid]
  null and void
volume ['vɔljum]
  volume of business/trade
voting ['voutiŋ]
  voting paper
  voting stock

wage(s *pl*) [weidʒ(iz)]
  minimum wage
  wage claim/earner
  wage increase
warehouse ['wɛəhaus]
  ex warehouse
  customs warehouse
warning ['wɔ:niŋ]
  to give s.o. fair warning
  without warning
wastage ['weistidʒ]
  wastage of food
waterproof ['wɔ:təpru:f]
way-bill ['weibil]
wear and tear ['wɛərən'tɛə]
weather ['weðə]
  weather conditions pl
  weather forecast
weekly ['wi:kli]
  weekly paper/report
  weekly wage
welfare work ['welfɛə]

wharf, *pl* **wharves** [wɔːf, wɔːvz]
white-collar worker ['waitˈkɔlə]
wholesale ['houl-seil]
   wholesale business/trade
   wholesale dealer, wholesaler
   wholesale price
winding-up ['waindiŋ'ʌp]
window ['windou]
   Inquire at window number three, please.
   window display
   window dresser
   window dressing
   window envelope
   window-shopping
wire ['waiə]
   by wire
wireless ['waiəlis]
   on the wireless
   wireless message
to withdraw [wiðˈdrɔː]
   He withdrew his motion.
   He wishes to withdraw his offer.
   to withdraw money from the bank
withdrawal [wiðˈdrɔːəl]
witness ['witnis]
word [wəːd]
   He heard by word of mouth.
wording ['wəːdiŋ]
work [wəːk]
   at work
   He is out of work.
   The computer is not working.
   clerical work
   piece work
   total work in hand
   work day
   workforce
   worker/workman
   workshop

   work to rule
working ['wəːkiŋ]
   working capital
   working clothes pl
   working conditions pl
   working cost/expenses pl
   working hour
world [wəːld]
   the business world
   World Bank
   world depression/economic crisis
   world economy/production
   world market
   world-wide
worth [wəːθ]
   worthless
to write off ['raitˈɔːf]
writing ['raitiŋ]
   to put in writing
   writing pad/paper
wrongful ['rɔŋful]
wrongly ['rɔŋli]

year [jəː]
   from year to year
   for years
   yearly
   financial/fiscal year
yield [jiːld]
   average yield
   tax yield
   The shares yielded a dividend of 10%.
   profit-yielding

zero, *pl* **zeros** ['ziərou, -z]
zip code *Am* ['zip koud]
zone [zoun]

Answer Key

II LETTERS ON BUSINESS SITUATIONS

1. Inquiries

Questions on the Letters

(a) Import inquiry (p. 12)

1. They deal in ladies' clothing.
2. They saw Grant & Clarkson's clothes at the London Fashion Show held in New York on October 17.
3. The 'Swinger' models would be most suitable for their market.
4. They want a quotation for spring and summer clothing that could be supplied by the end of January next. They want to know c.i.f. Chicago prices for a large number of dresses and suits in various sizes.

(b) Domestic inquiry (p. 13)

1. They read an advertisement in the 'Builders' Journal' of 3rd November.
2. They want a quotation for the new bathroom showers advertised.
3. They will place orders on condition that the equipment is of good quality and the offer is favourable.

(c) Export inquiry (p. 14)

1. Worldwide Dealers want quotations for 10,000 bicycles for delivery to Sri Lanka, India, Pakistan and Nepal.
2. They want to know what quantities can be delivered at regular intervals and the best terms for f.o.b. Brisbane.
3. The bicycles should be transported by container to Brisbane for onward shipment.

(d) Personal inquiry (p. 15)

1. She would like to buy a STIRTIP electric mixer for her niece.
2. She was told that they do not stock this make any more.
3. Mrs. Marks hopes that it is still obtainable from the manufacturers.

Exercises (p. 104)

1. It contains too few details for the supplier to make a proper quotation. He wants to know the quantity, type and what purpose the articles are needed for. It will also help the supplier to know when the customer wants delivery,

if he wants samples, or how he has heard of the products. In short: a fuller inquiry is more likely to result in an accurate quotation, without the need for additional correspondence.

2.

3rd August, 19___

Dear Sirs,

We are importers of foods and beverages, with outlets in Brazil and Venezuela. As we need approximately 200 cases of tea monthly, we would ask you to submit to us a special offer of Darjeeling tea. Your quotation should include your best prices, terms and delivery dates.

An early answer would be appreciated.

Yours faithfully,

---

2. Quotations, Offers

Questions on the Letters

(a) Export quotation: firm offer (p. 19)

1. The pink trouser suits in the smaller sizes have been sold out.
2. The other models could be supplied by the middle of January, subject to a firm order being received by 15th November.
3. Cuttings and a colour chart were sent by airmail on the morning of 30th October.

(b) Enclosing quotation (p. 21)

1. An illustrated catalogue is also enclosed.
2. Fittings which cannot be supplied from stock are marked with an asterisk. 4-6 weeks should be allowed for their delivery.
3. Building contractors have found the equipment easy to install and attractive in appearance.
4. A 2% trade discount is given on all orders of £600 and over, and 3% on orders over £2,000.
5. Shower A 42 includes a wall bracket.
6. Payment should be made net within 30 days of receiving the bill.

(c) Quoting terms for hotel accommodation (p. 22)

1. The receptionist says that they were pleased to hear that Mr. Yasni wishes to stay at the Atlantic Hotel again.
2. The cost of the midday and evening meals stays the same.
3. Accommodation is still available for June, and in May there are several double rooms free from the 23rd onwards and 3 single rooms from 26th May-3rd June.

1.

Dear Sirs,

Thank you very much for your inquiry of . . . . We are pleased to make you the following offer:

60,000 large clothes hooks (light metal in blue, green, gold)	£2,750
Terms of payment	30 days net

Enclosed are sample hooks in each of the colours requested and an order form. As regards delivery, we can dispatch the hooks immediately on receipt of the completed order form.

We look forward to receiving your order.

Yours faithfully,

Enc.

2.

10th August, 19__

Dear Sirs,

Thank you for your inquiry of 3rd August. As you requested, we are enclosing our latest price list and samples of our Darjeeling tea from Sri Lanka. We are sure that, after having compared it with other blends of tea, you will find our prices reasonable for this excellent quality of fine tea.

Our terms of payment are: cash against invoice for the first order.

Should you place further orders, we are willing to allow you three months' credit.

We look forward to receiving a trial order from you, which we shall execute promptly and carefully.

Yours faithfully,

Export Department

---

3. Sales Letters, Changes in Business

(a) Sales letter introducing product to a new market (p. 27)

1. English preserves have been regarded as the best for about 150 years.
2. People talk about them to their relatives, friends, and other prospective customers.

---

3. Some fruits come from English orchards and gardens, and citrus fruits are imported from Spain and Israel.

(b) Sales letter announcing company merger, offering a larger range of products and price reductions (p. 28)

1. They have decided to merge in order to obtain closer co-operation and rationalization of production.
2. A larger range of cameras, projectors and optical equipment will be available, and the customer can also expect price reductions.
3. Universal Nikko Optics want to maintain the personal relationship, and to continue the prompt service that their customers are used to.

Exercises (p. 104)

1.

---

19 March 19___

Dear Sirs,

Thank you for the letter you wrote us last month. Please excuse the delay in replying, caused by my absence from the office on urgent business matters.

I agree with you that the fall in sales, which you have also noticed, is very worrying. However, I would like to assure you that our company has continued to make every effort to promote sales and to interest customers in the 'Superfax A 5'. On examining the possible causes, we here think that the decline may be due to the recent price increase, and more competition from other manufacturers of copying machines. Another reason, as we reported to you previously, may be due to some customers having found defects in your machines, which has not improved sales either.

In our opinion it would be a good time now to introduce new products. For this some effective measures are needed on your part.

If you wish we are willing to give you further details of such measures. In the meantime we would like to hear your opinion, and would therefore ask you to let us have your comments. We look forward to hearing from you soon.

Yours faithfully,

Sales Manager

2.

Dear Sir(s),

We have pleasure in announcing that we are opening a new factory on 1st September in Springvale, Scotland. Here we shall produce skis of

---

145

glass fibre reinforced with plastic, a special polyester which provides maximum elasticity and strength.

Originally we had planned to make ski poles of plastic, too. However, tests revealed that this material was not quite suitable. We have thus arranged collaboration with the British Light Alloy Company of Brixton, where the ski poles are to be manufactured of special light metal conical tube.

As a result we are able to make you a unique offer of skis and poles at special introductory prices. These are shown on the price list enclosed. We know you will want to take advantage of this offer, and are looking forward to receiving your order.

Yours faithfully,

CONTINENTAL SPORTS COMPANY LTD.

4. Counter-Proposals, Concessions

Questions on the Letters (p. 31)

(a) Counter-proposal

1. Brazilian buyers are used to a jar containing 500 grammes, whereas the English pound is only 454 grammes.
2. They ask for a 10% price reduction.
3. They suggest payment of half the invoice amount on receipt of the goods, and the second half within 30 days, less 2% discount.

(b) Reply to counter-proposal (p. 32)

1. They think Roberts Import Company's customers will notice and appreciate the superior quality.
2. They are willing to allow a special discount of 5% on 15,000 jars, plus a 2% cash discount.

Exercises (p. 105)

1.

> 17 August, 19__
>
> Dear Sirs,
>
> Thank you for your price list and the samples you sent us on 10th August. Compared with other teas, the quality is indeed higher, but so are your prices, particularly in the face of increased competition from new areas of tea production in Africa.

Could you reduce your prices by 20% so that we can make a special introductory offer? Once our customers have bought the tea and after they have tasted it—there will be a much better chance of selling it at regular prices.

Yours faithfully,

5. Orders, Order Acknowledgements

Questions on the Letters

(b) Enclosing an acknowledgement (p. 37)

1. FARMERS enclose a signed copy of Roberts Import Company's order as an acknowledgement.
2. FARMERS' dispatch department will let Roberts Import Company know when the marmalade is due to arrive.
3. FARMERS write a letter out of politeness, to wish Roberts Import Company a good turnover and to indicate that they are looking forward to repeat orders.

(d) Import order (p. 39)

1. The most popular sizes are 10, 12 and 14.
2. Delivery should be made by air freight, c.i.f. Chicago.
3. Matthews & Wilson will open a letter of credit with Grant & Clarkson's bank.
4. The dresses are needed in time for Christmas.

(e) Exchange of cables (p. 39)

1. The order says 2100 'Swinger' dresses, but the specification only adds up to 1900.
2. It is probably a mistake in calculation: the order was not properly checked.
3. Both the buyer and the supplier want to know quite clearly what quantity is to be supplied. Cables are not signed, so it is best to confirm them by letter.

(f) Confirmation (p. 40)

1. The letter refers to the discrepancy between the first paragraph of Matthews & Wilson's order, i.e. 2100 'Swinger' dresses, and the specification amounting to 1900.
2. Cables sometimes contain errors. It is wise to repeat them in the letter of confirmation.

3. The goods can be dispatched as soon as confirmation is received that a letter of credit has been opened.

4. The original quotation of 30th October was for sea freight. Air cargo, which saves time, is more expensive, so the customer will have to pay the extra costs.

Exercises (p. 105)

1.

29th August, 19___

Dear Sirs,

Thank you for allowing us a price concession. We confidently hope this will result in increased sales to our mutual advantage.

We now order
     150 cases of Darjeeling tea, No. 412
for immediate delivery.

May we ask you for a credit of three months? Please let us have your order acknowledgement by return.

Yours faithfully,

2.

5th September, 19___

Dear Sirs,

We were very pleased to receive your order for 150 cases of our No. 412 Darjeeling tea. We shall be able to execute the order by the end of this month.

You asked us to grant you three months credit. As we pointed out in our letter of 10th August, for this initial order our terms are cash against invoice. We enclose a pro-forma invoice and look forward to an early reply.

Yours faithfully,

---

6. Dispatch, Packing, Transport

Questions on the Letters

(a) Advice of dispatch (p. 42)

    1. It was dispatched by rail.
    2. It will be shipped from Southampton (MV Orion) to Sao Paulo.

3. Its destination is Sao Paulo.
4. An invoice contains the names of the supplier and the customer, date, details of order (order number, date), quantity, description and price of goods, details of delivery, packing, marks, terms of payment, discounts.

(b) Packing (p. 43)

1. They are then to be shipped overseas from Brisbane.
2. A container holds a large quantity. Once packed, the contents need no handling until the container reaches its destination. The packing of the goods can be light.
3. The seller pays for freight until the goods are on board at Brisbane. The buyer pays the rest, or may charge it to his customer.
4. Container hire will be charged to Worldwide Dealers Ltd.

(c) Air shipment (p. 44)

1. Credit was only confirmed on the 19th.
2. The original quotation of 30th October was for sea freight. Air freight is more expensive, so the customer was charged extra.
3. Besides the usual shipping documents (invoice, packing lists, insurance certificate or policy), an air shipment requires an air waybill and often a certificate of origin.

Exercises (p. 106)

1.

August 7, 19___

Gentlemen:

On behalf of the Worldwide Dealers of Hong Kong, we are attaching a specification of delivery instructions for the 42 containers of bicycles. These are to be addressed to our Madras warehouse (address as above) and marked according to the specifications.

Please let us have a consular invoice and certificate of origin besides the usual commercial invoices.

Very truly yours,

Enc.

2.

17th August, 19___

Dear Sirs,

We are pleased to inform you that the 42 containers of bicycles were dispatched to you this morning according to the delivery instructions contained in your letter of 7th August.

As requested, we enclose a consular invoice and certificate of origin, together with our invoice.

We look forward to hearing from you on receipt of the bicycles.

Yours faithfully,

Enclosures

7. Payment and Reminders

Questions on the Letters

(a) Making payment (p. 49)

1. Carsons pay by cheque (check).
2. Carsons are pleased with the way the order was carried out, since the furniture arrived exactly on time.

(b) Acknowledging payment

1. Carsons' account is now completely clear.
2. They enclose a receipt.

(c) Reminder (p. 50)

1. Payment was about a week overdue when the reminder was written.
2. They should disregard the reminder.

(d) Second notice (p. 51)

1. They are writing because the Mandarin Importing & Exporting Co. still have not settled their account.
2. They are prepared to wait another two weeks.

(e) Final notice

1. It is direct and impersonal, without being impolite, ending with a threat of legal action.
2. They should have sent a check by now, or at least have explained the delay in payment.
3. Other suppliers of customers could hear of it, either direct or through a credit inquiry agency.

(f) Request for extension of credit (p. 52)

1. There was a fire at their warehouse, which caused excessive losses.
2. They think they will need another three months (from the date of the letter) to pay off the balance.

(g) Extending credit (p. 53)

    1. They understand the difficulty and are willing to grant the extension of payment asked for.

    2. They ask Bunbury Estate Builders to sign a 90-day promissory note.

(h) Refusing extension (p. 54)

    1. Bunbury Estate Builders have asked for an extension of credit several times in the past.

    2. They will place the account in the hands of a collection agency.

    3. A collection agency can first ask for payment by a certain date, and if this is not made, can take legal steps to recover the debt.

Exercises (p. 106)

1.(a)

Gentlemen:

We refer to your invoice No. 431826 of January 2, due for payment on February 15.

Unfortunately trade has been very slack recently. Customers who usually buy our products in large numbers during the winter have been very hesitant in their purchases, probably due to a general uncertainty prevalent in our branch recently.

We would like to make you a proposal for extended terms of credit. With this letter we are enclosing a check for one third of the amount due, namely $3,260; the balance can be paid by April 30. We do hope you can agree to this proposal, and look forward to your confirmation.

                                    Sincerely yours,

(b) (p. 106)

                              15th November, 19___

Dear Sirs,

On 13th October you wrote to us confirming receipt of the shipment of Darjeeling tea. As you remember from our previous correspondence, our terms of payment were cash against invoice, i.e. the amount was due to be paid by 15th October.

As we have no record of having received your remittance, we would ask you to settle the overdue account by return.

                                  Yours faithfully,

Questions on the Letters

(a) Complaint (p. 57)

1. The red dresses, size 12, are lighter in colo(u)r than those in the other sizes.
2. A collection of various sizes is delivered to each store.
3. They ask them to replace the whole lot by 100 dresses, size 12, in the correct colour.
4. Costs for packing (which is lighter for air freight) and insurance (which is also less for a shorter period of time) must have been less for air cargo than for sea/land shipment.
5. They want the invoice amount reduced.

(b) Handling a complaint (p. 58)

1. The colour was overlooked by the controller responsible.
2. They are sending a new lot by air, and ask Matthews & Wilson to return the faulty clothes, carriage forward, or to keep them for sales as seconds at a reduced price.
3. In this case there was no reduction in packing or insurance costs compared with sea freight.

(c) Answering a complaint about poor service (p. 59)

1. She complained about the unsatisfactory service she experienced when her washing machine had to be repaired.
2. Because of illness he came later than arranged.
3. Mrs. Brien was not informed that the repairman would call on Monday.
4. The Service Engineer will personally see to it that she is not kept waiting if she needs repairs in future.

Exercises

1. (a) (p. 106)

---

18 December, 19___

Dear Sirs,

You advised us in your letter of 28 November that we would receive the latest shipment of Darjeeling tea within the first week of December. However it has still not arrived at Sao Paulo.

Would you please look into this non-delivery, let us have your explanation, and inform us when we may expect the tea.

Yours faithfully,

(b)

> 23rd December, 19＿
>
> Dear Sirs,
>
> As soon as we received your letter of 18th December we took up the matter with our forwarding agents. The cases of tea are still in transit, and we have instructed our forwarders to get them to you this week if possible.
>
> We apologize for the inconvenience that this delay must have caused you.
>
> Yours faithfully,

III LETTERS ON SOCIAL SITUATIONS

1. Appointments and Travel Arrangements

Questions on the Letters

(a) Making an appointment (p. 63)

1. He mentioned it in his letter of 9 August.
2. He suggests any time on Thursday, 4 September.
3. Mr. Carter should leave a message at Mr. Hanna's hotel, saying what time would suit him.
4. One of the most important matters is the percentage of commission the International Import Corporation should receive for distributing Business Machines Ltd.'s SELECT copier in Egypt.

(b) Expressing regret at having missed someone (p. 64)

1. Mr. Johansson was expecting him on 5th April, not on 3rd April.
2. She gave him some of the data he required.

(c) Travel arrangements to be made (p. 65)

1. It is difficult for him to make travel arrangements from the USSR.
2. He asks her to type a draft of his notes, to make hotel and travel bookings, to wire a confirmation to him at his hotel in Istanbul.

(d) Travel arrangements made (p. 66)

1. He leaves on flight BA 109 at 17.00.
2. He will stay at the Hotel Ambassador, where a single room has been booked for him.
3. There was no seat available on the direct flight.

Exercises

1. (a) (p. 107)

Dear Sirs,

It was very kind of you to offer to place a car at my disposal for my
forthcoming business trip to England. As I have already mentioned,
I shall be arriving at London Airport on Flight LH 712 at 10.15 a.m.
on 14 January, and after calling on you, plan to spend two more days
in London. On 17 January I shall be visiting suppliers in East Anglia,
the Midlands and the West Country, which should take me about
two weeks.

Would you kindly let me know what expenses are likely to arise for
petrol, maintenance, liability and other insurance. Perhaps you would
prefer me to pay a certain amount depending on the mileage I do. I
expect to travel about 200 to 300 miles per week.

I should appreciate having this information before my departure next
week. With many thanks in advance, I am

Yours sincerely,

Fernando Suarez

(b) (p. 107)

29 August 19___

Dear, Mr. Johannsen,

As you know, I shall be attending the business meeting you are
having at your head office on Thursday and Friday, 26 and 27
September next. I look forward to seeing you again on this occasion,
and to meeting other members of your staff.

This will be my first visit to Denmark, and I should also like to travel
privately during the week-end following the meeting. I wonder if
you could give me some recommendations on coach and train trips.

I'd appreciate any help you can give me in this matter.
Thank you.

Yours sincerely,

Frank Swann

Questions on the Letters

(f) Inviting a guest speaker (p. 74)

1. They are writing to ask him to be their guest speaker at a luncheon to be held in Singapore on September 21.
2. They offer to pay his travelling expenses and two days' accommodation in Singapore, as well as a fee of $400.

Exercises

1. (a) (p. 107)

---

23 January 19___

Dear Mr. Diaz,

It would give me great pleasure if you could come to Mexico City for a week-end this spring, in order to give two talks to teachers of English. We plan to hold a seminar for those teachers whose subject is English for business purposes, e.g. business letter and report writing, and for teachers at our university. As possible subjects I would suggest

The importance of report writing
English for business purposes: is translation really necessary?

We should like to hold the meeting on 27/28 March, and hope you will be able to accept this invitation.

Yours sincerely,

(b)

---

3 February 19___

Dear Professor,

I was very pleased to hear from you again, and to know that you are still engaged in in-service of language teachers.

It would give me great pleasure to attend your week-end seminar on 27/28 March. I would be able to speak on either of the subjects you suggest. The second one, 'English for business purposes: is translation really necessary?' would, in fact, lend itself well to a panel discussion with four of five practising teachers taking part.

I look forward to receiving fuller details of the programme in due course, and especially to seeing you again in March.

Sincerely

Carla Diaz

Questions on the Letters

(a) Thanks for hospitality: request (business) (p. 77)

1. Mr. Hakka is in the life assurance (insurance) business in Tokyo.
2. His management is interested in the activities of the Anglo-Thai Insurance Company.
3. They can follow their activities by reading the annual report and accounts each year.
4. This is a list of addresses of people who want to receive information regularly by mail (price lists, reports, or other publications).

(b) Complying with a request (p. 78)

1. The full report is published in Thai only.
2. They are sending a copy of the report in Thai, plus a short version in English.
3. They want to know which version he would like to receive in future.

Exercises

1. (a) (p. 107)

---

15 May 19__

Dear Sir or Madam,

I have been given the name of your school by my English teacher. Would you please send me a prospectus and details of your fees. I am interested in attending a 2-month course in English (intermediate level) next summer from 20th June to 18th August.

Can you arrange for me to live with a family during the course? I am 19 years old, have just finished my training as a draughtsman, and my interests are sports—especially soccer—and photography. Naturally I would be willing to share a room with a student of another nationality (not Spanish speaking), so that we can practise talking English in our spare time.

Thank you in advance for any help you can give me.

Yours faithfully,

(b)

Dear Mr. Fellowes,

Having returned home after a most interesting stay at Oxford, I would like to thank you again for the fine opportunity you gave me

---

to extend my training in your company. Although there are, of course, many similarities in systems of car engine assembly in both our factories, I was able to observe and learn several new methods that will certainly be useful in my work here. Even today I was able to show our foreman how it was possible to economize on time in fitting a fuel pump.

I certainly won't forget the personal contacts I was able to make during my short stay, and the kindness shown me by yourself and the members of your staff.

Yours sincerely,

4. Employment: Applications, Letters of Recommendation, Giving Notice

Questions on the Letters

Advertisement (p. 81)

1. They will take part in a six months' induction and field training scheme.
2. They can look forward to a company car, expenses, a pension fund, life insurance, sickness benefits and generous holidays.
3. Applicants need to have a university degree.
4. The applicant should write or telephone, and a meeting can be arranged near his home.

(a) Application (p. 83)

1. He has been working in pharmaceuticals and cosmetics, but he believes that industrial products offer greater potential.
2. He has a university degree in chemistry.
3. He has attended an evening course in Marketing, and he has sales experience.
4. He has to give one month's notice in his present position, and thus could start with Avery one month after being offered a job.

(b) Confirming employment (p. 84)

1. Mr. Ryder must have indicated his willingness to accept the position during his telephone conversation with the personnel manager on August 10. Now he should sign both copies of the contract of employment and return them.
2. They are explained in the contract of employment.
3. Also enclosed is information about the superannuation fund, staff canteen, sports and social club, other facilities and fringe benefits.
4. He should contact the personnel manager's office.
5. He will start his training on October 1.

(c) Contract of employment (p. 86)

1. He would not be paid extra, but if he worked overtime at the request of W & T Avery, he could take four hours' time off.
2. These are public holidays, such as Christmas, Easter, and bank holidays, e.g. in August and May (Britain), or Labour Day, Thanksgiving (USA).
3. He would have to give one month's notice.
4. The company encourages its employees to join a trade union, but the final decision is left to the individual.
5. One should complain to the head of department.

(d) Giving notice

1. This is one of the terms of his employment contract.
2. He wants to extend his professional activities to a wider field of industry.
3. This is an important letter, by which he terminates his employment. A registered letter gives him proof of having posted it, and of the recipient having received it before the beginning of September.

Exercises (p. 107)

1. (a) We have a vacancy in our Personnel Department for an assistant.

> For this interesting job you need
> a liking for personal contact
> experience in correspondence and documentation.

> You would help the personnel manager in
> seeking employees
> personnel selection
> in-service training.

> If you would like to know more, we would like to know you. Please apply to:

The Personnel Manager
Box A 1802
The Guardian
Manchester

15 December 19___

Dear Sir,

With reference to your advertisement in yesterday's 'Guardian', I would like to apply for the post of personnel assistant.

I was struck by the fact that your first requirement for the applicant was a liking for personal contact. I have always looked for this in my profession; as a social worker in Manchester for the last two years I have had many opportunities to gain the kind of experience you are looking for. I have helped in career selection, compiling personal

---

record sheets and keeping documentation up to date, although I have not had many opportunities for correspondence.

My reason for seeking employment in business or industry is the prospect of earning a higher salary. As I am planning to get married, I am looking for a job where I can earn an adequate salary.

Please let me know if and when I may come for an interview. I would very much like to know more about this job.

Yours faithfully,

Peter Burns

(c)

24 December 19___

Dear Mr. Hampshire,

Thank you for inviting me to your office and telling me so much about the post as your assistant. I would like to confirm what I said after our meeting: that I accept the job you offered.

Meanwhile I have spoken to my present employer, who will release me from my present job at the end of the year. I have now given notice, and will be able to start working for your company on 5th January 19___.

Please accept my best wishes for Christmas and the New Year.

Yours sincerely,

Peter Burns

(d)

24 December 19___

Dear Sir,

Thank you for offering me a position as a clerk in your company. Although it seems very attractive, I have decided to accept another job which, I believe, is more suitable with regard to my qualifications.

Therefore I must decline.

Yours faithfully,

Peter Burns

2. (p. 108)

June 20th, 19___

Dear Sir,

I should like to inform you that I wish to terminate my employment
with the company on July 31st, 19___. According to the terms of my
contract, I am required to give one month's notice.

For the past two years I have been employed as a technical translator,
and although Bensons has always treated me well, I am afraid that I
am beginning to find the work itself rather monotonous. There also
seems little chance of advancement from my present position.

Thus I feel that I should accept the offer I have just received of a
position with an engineering firm in Teheran.

Yours faithfully,

Denise Bevan

5. Goodwill Letters: Congratulations, Introductions, Condolence, Christmas and New Year Wishes

Questions on the Letters

(a) Goodwill letter (p. 90)

   1. They have been doing business together for ten years.
   2. Bonds appreciates Alexiou Shipping Company's regular custom.
   3. They appreciate the service Bonds offers.

(b) Congratulations (p. 91)

   1. He congratulates Mr. Lyons on his appointment as Regional Manager for
      the Middle East.
   2. He has both enthusiasm and experience.
   3. Mr. Wetherby's colleagues also send their congratulations.

(c) Introducing a business friend (p. 92)

   1. Mr. Kamthon is a friend of Mr. Saxer's, and is studying Economics at
      Chulalongkorn University.
   2. He plans to enter the insurance business in a few months' time.
   3. In the meantime he is making a study trip to Japan in order to contribute
      towards a book which is in preparation entitled 'Social Insurance Abroad'.

4. He asks Mr. Hakka to see Mr. Kamthon or give him an introduction to someone on his staff.

(d) Asking for introductions (p. 93)

1. He would like some introductions from Mr. Wembley, as he and his wife are going to Delhi, where Mr. Wembley has lived for several years.
2. He may need them for business, and his wife would like to get to know some people, as she may feel lonely at times.
3. He asks Mr. Wembley if there is anything he can do for him, either in the States or in Delhi.

(e) Condolence (p. 94)

1. He served on the Museum Board for a long time.
2. He was grateful for Mr. Williams' sound judgement and advice.
3. They offer their condolences to members of Mr. Williams' family.

(f) Get-well wishes (p. 95)

1. He became ill suddenly.
2. Their business can be settled when Mr. Sukarman is well again.

(g) Seasonal wishes (p. 96)

1. They are writing to all their friends and customers.
2. They thank them for their continued confidence and patronage.
3. They wish them a prosperous New Year.

Exercises (p. 108)

1. (a)

Dear Walter,

I recently met Harry Stanford, who told me that you had been appointed as sales manager at A & S Industries.

Having worked together with you so long, I can confidently say that you are the right man in the right position. Your enterprise and enthusiasm, coupled with your co-operative attitude towards staff and customers alike, are certainly the qualities to stand you in good stead for your new responsibilities.

Please accept my congratulations.

Sincerely,

Martin Rutherford

(b)

2 June 19___

Dear Mr. Hampshire,

We at the office were very sorry to hear that your recent illness has taken a bad turn, and that you have had to be moved to hospital. However, I am sure you will be able to have the treatment there that you need, and hope this will lead to a speedy recovery.

Things here are continuing smoothly; Mr. Church looks into the department from time to time to clear up any matters I cannot deal with on my own.

As time may seem to pass slowly, we of the personnel department are sending you a book, which we think you will enjoy reading. All the staff join me in hoping you will get well soon.

IV TELEGRAMS, TELEX MESSAGES

Exercises (p. 108)

1. (a)

NO ACKNOWLEDGEMENT RECEIVED FOR ORDER 50 PAIRS VOGUE SHOES 21 APRIL STOP REQUIRED 14 JUNE LATEST STOP WIRE DELIVERY TIME

(b)

Evans & Donaldson Inc.
Louisville, Kentucky 40201

Continental Tooling Service
19 West Fourth Street
Dayton, Ohio 45401   August 25, 19___

Subject: Order No. 912

Gentlemen:

This morning we sent you the following telex:

    contooling 658 31029 1973-8.20
    shipment order 912 due yesterday unreceived stop
    will return goods if not delivered by august 28
    evdonson

If you refer to our order, you will see that it was placed on condition that the goods were at our warehouse here in Dayton by August 24. We have promised our customers delivery by September 3, and your delay is causing us considerable difficulties.

We do hope that, in accordance with our telex request, the goods are now underway. They are urgently required, and we will have to consider the order cancelled if we do not have them by August 28.

Very truly yours,
Evans & Donaldson Inc.